GW00644898

少年の日本語

japanese for teens

"There are only three ways to learn Japanese: practice, practice, and practice."

- J.R. Maroney Sensei

Table of Contents

japanese for teens

Edition 1 Revision 10
Register of Copyrights, United States of America: TX-7-483-423

ISBN 978-0-9778926-3-1 (paper)

This copy released via Lulu Press
3131 RDU Center, Suite 210
Morrisville, NC 27560
www.lulu.com

Why Should I Learn Japanese?

Firstly, you should not learn Japanese because you think all Japanese are rich and that knowing Japanese will instantly make you rich or successful in business—this is simply not the case. I learned about the Japanese from my grandfather who served in the occupation army immediately after World War II. Even in the early seventies, my grandfather knew that the Japanese were masters of manufacturing and would someday make all TV's, electronics, cars, and who knew what else. Much of what he predicted has come true and listening to his tales sparked an interest in Japan and the Japanese language that stays with me today. I attempted to learn Japanese on my own at the age of 16. Unfortunately, at that time effective study materials were scarce, and many text books used romanji (alphabet letters) to teach Japanese so my efforts quickly turned to frustration. After arriving in Japan at the age of 19 I realized that the romanji method was actually detrimental, and that the Japanese in text books was very different from the actual language spoken in Japan. This is why I encourage students to learn the hiragana first, and this text uses only hiragana and simple kanji. Once in Japan I was forced to learn all of the hiragana, and my language ability improved at an amazing pace. I was fluent within six months of study.

Since then, I've taught Japanese all over the world, mostly to teens who want to understand Manga and Anime in its native language. While teaching these young adults, I struggled to find text books that fit their unique needs so I created this book. Furthermore, this workbook has been written so you too can easily pick up the basics by including only the most effective methods for learning Japanese; something I've learned from many years of teaching the Japanese language.

Besides allowing you to connect to a nation of 130 million people in their native tongue, Japanese will help you think about things in a different way. I like to say that it adds a third dimension to thinking. The Japanese language is also intertwined with Japanese culture, helping one to understand why the Japanese do what they do. In fact, there are words in Japanese, like, "Otsukare sama desu," that simply don't exist in English. Native English speakers often comment that Japanese is the world's most difficult language to learn when in reality, Japanese only seems difficult because Japanese is a vocabulary based language while English is a grammar based language (check the thickness of each dictionary!)

How is Japanese for Teens different?

Japanese is a constantly changing language, and teenagers in Japan are a driving force behind this phenomenon. For example, the 1,423-page, 2009 edition, of Gendai Yogo no Kiso Chisiki (Encyclopedia of Contemporary Words) has five pages of new terms created by teens, many of which are contractions of common words. I think of teens in Japan as sparks that ignite new trends in fashion, food, expression, and language – trends that often spread globally. The worlds of Anime and Manga are no different and the language used often in these media is often very "teenager." These trends are not something a native English speaker can learn easily outside of Japan. However, this workbook helps the native English speaker not only learn the basics of modern Japanese, but also become familiar with new expressions encountered in Anime, Manga, and other types of media.

JR's principles for learning Japanese:

- Enjoy it! – Japanese stayed with me because I always had fun with it.
- Learn the culture simultaneously – Meet Japanese, watch Anime, learn about this unique and fascinating culture.
- Think in Japanese – To be fluent, your thoughts must be in Japanese.

How does the system work?

Each lesson consists of three sections: Vocabulary, Grammar, and Practice. Initially, all students are expected to learn the basic 46 hiragana characters before starting lesson one. As mentioned, learning the hiragana is critical for understanding Japanese pronunciations. Vocabulary should be studied and mastered at the start of each lesson. Review of vocabulary for previous sections is also crucial. Furthermore, students are given the opportunity to practice what they have learned by creating Manga stories. Also, modern devices like laptop computers, cell phones, etc., can be used to help students practice vocabulary.

Learning Japanese in Japan is ideal, but not possible for everyone. Therefore, I've employed techniques that simulate the experience of learning in Japan. This is a work constantly changing in a constantly changing world; your suggestions for improvements are greatly appreciated.

***Anime terms are usually drawn from local dialects, made-up words, and street slang. These words should never be used when conversing with Japanese people; they are presented here as a way for the student to comprehend Anime text and video for viewing only.**

Studying Japanese will improve your English skills.

Japanese grammar is often opposite of English. By understanding how Japanese grammar works, students get a better idea of the basic grammar structures for all languages. As you learn about Japanese grammar rules, think about their counterparts in English.

Using this workbook

- Because students are not expected to know kanji at this point, nouns are highlighted in yellow. Therefore, we strongly suggest purchasing the color version.
- Key words are underlined to help you distinguish them in a sentence.
- Because this is a workbook, students are encouraged to write in the book. And because students are expected to write in the book, we discourage the purchase of used versions.

がんばってください！

J. R. Maroney

Yes, you may write in this book !

every tall building needs a strong foundation

LEARNING HIRAGANA

The best way to learn the Hiragana is to practice writing them, and a good way to remember them initially is through association. Below we have provided associations designed to help native English speakers learn Japanese Hiragana quickly. Using a pencil, lightly outline the characters listed under "Stroke Order." The order of the stroke is marked with small numbers which are placed at the beginning of the stroke. It is important to write the Hiragana using the proper stroke order. Then, use the "Practice" cells to practice writing the characters. If you need more room, use the blank pages at the end of this section and in the back of the book. NOTE: The associations here are in no way related to the meaning of the Hiragana characters; rather, they are only presented as a way to help you memorize the shape of the character.

Hiragana	Sound	Stroke Order	Association	Practice		
あ	A	あ SAIL BOAT	あ SAIL BOAT	あ	あ	あ
い	I	い	い CHOPSTICKS	い	い	い
う	U	う	う RABBIT	う	う	う
え	E	え	え PRAYING MANTIS	え	え	え
お	O	お	お ANCHOR	お	お	お
か	KA	か	か WATERFALL	か	か	か
き	KI	き	き TREE	き	き	き

く	KU	く	く KITE			
け	KE	け	け SCROLL			
こ	KO	こ	こ UFO			
さ	SA	さ	さ MONKEY			
し	SHI	し	し FISH HOOK			
す	SU	す	す NEEDLE + THREAD			
せ	SE	せ	せ CHAIR			
そ	SO	そ	そ HAIRPIN			
た	TA	た	た SOLAR PANEL			
ち	CHI	ち	ち SPOON			

つ	TSU	つ	 つ WAVE (TSUNAMI)			
て	TE	て	 て TABLE			
と	TO	と	 と WHALE			
な	NA	な	 な PITCHER POURING WATER			
に	NI	に	 に BUTTERFLY			
ぬ	NU	ぬ	 ぬ NOODLE BOWL			
ね	NE	ね	 ね CAT			
の	NO	の	 の MOUSE			
は	HA	は	 は SUSPENSION BRIDGE			
ひ	HI	ひ	 ひ CLOWN			

ふ	FU	ふ	 ふ GHOST			
へ	HE	へ	 へ MOUNTAIN			
ほ	HO	ほ	 ほ MUSIC NOTE			
ま	MA	ま	 ま ま TELEPHONE POLE			
み	MI	み	 み CURSIVE "H"			
む	MU	む	 む COFFEE MUG			
め	ME	め	 め ROCK			
も	MO	も	 も FISH HOOK + WORM			
ら	RA	ら	 ら GOLF CLUB			
り	RI	り	 り SKIS			

る	RU	る	る KANGAROO WITH BABY			
れ	RE	れ	れ FISHING POLE + HOOK			
ろ	RO	ろ	ろ KANGAROO			
や	YA	や	や KITE			
ゆ	YU	ゆ	ゆ FISH			
よ	YO	よ	よ FLAG POST			
わ	WA	わ	わ FROG			
を	WO	を	を HORSE-RIDER			
ん	N	ん	ん NEEDLE + THREAD			

HERE'S SOME HELP WITH PRONUNCIATION:

A あ is pronounced like the "a" in amend or apply.
I い is pronounced like the "e" in me or be.
U う is pronounced like the "u" in super.
E え is pronounced like the "a" in pay or may.
O お is pronounced like the "o" in poke or joke.

WHAT ABOUT THE SOUNDS FOR G, Z, D, AND B?

To make the sounds for G (GA, GI, GU, GE, GO), we add two small strokes to the upper right corner of KA, KI, KU, KE, KO. These strokes are most often referred to as "ten-ten."

か	き	く	け	こ
が	ぎ	ぐ	げ	ご

Repeat for S (SA, SHI, SU, SE, SO) → Z (ZA, JI*, ZU, ZE, ZO)、

さ	し	す	せ	そ
ざ	じ	ず	ぜ	ぞ

*JI is pronounced like "Je" in Jeep

Repeat for T → D、

た	ち	つ	て	と
だ	ぢ	づ	で	ど

*ぢ (CHI ten-ten) is pronounced the same as じ but is rarely used. づ (ZU) is pronounced the same as ず but is rarely used.

Repeat for H → B、

は	ひ	ふ	へ	ほ
ば	び	ぶ	べ	ぼ

Finally, to get the P sound (PA, PI, PU, PE, PO), add a small circle (maru) to the upper right corner of the corresponding character in H,

は	ひ	ふ	へ	ほ
ぱ	ぴ	ぷ	ぺ	ぽ

USE THE FOLLOWING SPACE TO PRACTICE WRITING HIRAGANA

* Now that you are familiar with the Hiragana, take the practice test in Appendix A without looking at the answers above. Make sure you know the Hiragana that you miss before you go on.

LESSON 1 VOCABULARY : BASIC EXPRESSIONS

Now that you are comfortable with Hiragana, let's learn some basic expressions.

Good Morning	おはようございます　おはよう (anime)
Good Afternoon	こんにちは
Good Evening	こんばんは
Thank You	（どうも）ありがとうございます ありがとう (anime)
Excuse me	すみません
You're Welcome	どういたしまして
Goodbye (for Boy)	さようなら (formal)　またね (anime)
Goodbye (for Girl)	さようなら (formal)　じゃね (anime)
(say) before a meal	いただきます
(say) after a meal	ごちそうさまでした
Yes, that is so	ええ、そうです　うん！(anime)
No, that is not correct	いいえ、ちがいます そうじゃなくて (anime)
Where is it?	どこですか　どこ？ (anime)
I'm home!	ただいま
Welcome home!	おかえりなさい　おかえり！ (anime)
I'm going now!	いってきます
See you later! (family's response to いってきます	いってらっしゃい
One O'clock	いちじです
To Be (the verb, 'is')	です
Name	なまえ
Nice to meet you	はじめまして
Homework	しゅくだい

MY NOTES:

JR's Advice
Want to learn Japanese faster? Think in Japanese! During the day, use the above phrases in your head and before long, these words will become second nature

LESSON 1 GRAMMAR : NUMBERS

You will need a good grasp of the number system before telling time. Practice Japanese numbers from 1 to 100 forward and backward.

1	いち		11	じゅういち
2	に		12	じゅうに
3	さん		13	じゅうさん
4	し	よん	14	じゅうよん
5	ご		15	じゅうご
6	ろく		16	じゅうろく
7	しち	なな	17	じゅうなな
8	はち		18	じゅうはち
9	く	きゅう	19	じゅうきゅう
10	じゅう		20	にじゅう

21	にじゅういち	31 さんじゅういち
22	にじゅうに	40 よんじゅう
23	にじゅうさん	50 ごじゅう
24	にじゅうし	55 ごじゅうご
25	にじゅうご	60 ろくじゅう
26	にじゅうろく	67 ろくじゅうなな
27	にじゅうしち	72 ななじゅうに
28	にじゅうはち	88 はちじゅうはち
29	にじゅうく	93 きゅうじゅうさん
30	さんじゅう	100 ひゃく

Notice
さんじゅうに
3 x 10 + 2 = 32

MY NOTES:

LESSON 1 GRAMMAR: TELLING TIME

With just a few key vocabulary words, you can tell time in Japanese

O'clock = じ Now = いま A.M = ごぜん P.M. = ごご

Add です for the formal ....じです

Example: 1 o'clock = いちじです。 **2 o'clock=**にじです。

9 o'clock=くじです。 **11 o'clock=**じゅういちじです。

You try: （**Write the time in Japanese below the clock**）

____________________ ____________________

Half past the hour = はん

Minutes are denoted ふん **or** ぷん **as follows:**

いっぷん、にふん、さんぷん、よんぷん、ごふん、ろっぷん、ななふん、はっぷん、きゅうふん、じゅっぷん。

Example: 9:13am = ごぜんくじじゅうさんぷんです。

Example: 7:30pm = ごごしちじはんです。

What time is it now? = いまはなんじですか

NOTE:
The は in いまはなんじですか is actually pronounced "wa." This は is a particle and will be covered in the next lesson.

FYI: There is no 's (apostrophe s) in Japanese. This is why each minute has its own "counter." We will learn more in Lesson 7.

LESSON 1: PRACTICE

Write the correct time in Japanese

4:00

8:00

10:30

5:30

5:40

3:35

8:40

9:55

7:33

2:22

1:11

A.M. To designate a.m., add ごぜん before the time. Ex: 5:00am = ごぜんごじ

P.M. To designate p.m., add ごご before the time. Ex: 5:00pm = ごごごじ

11:37 am

6:18 pm

12:44 am

Practice on your own, answer the question in Japanese:

What time is it right now?

What time do you go to bed?

What time do you wake up?

What time were you born?

What time does school/work end?

LESSON 2: VOCABULARY

	Japanese (日本語)	Anime (アニメ)
Me, I	わたし	ぼく (Boy)
You	あなた	きみ・おまえ
Clock, Watch	とけい	
Pen	ぺん	
Pencil	えんぴつ	
Bag	かばん	
Friend	ともだち	
Desk	つくえ	
Chair	いす	
Book	ほん	
Mother	おかあさん	
Building	たてもの	
Hospital	びょういん	
Book Store	ほんや	
Car	くるま	
School	がっこう	
Room	へや	
Train	でんしゃ	

NOTE:
You may hear the words きみ and おまえ in Anime; however, please do not use these words as they may be insulting. You will learn more about levels of politeness in lessons 6 through 12.
JR せんせい

	Adjectives:	Critical Verbs:	
White	しろ・しろい	To be, "is"	です
Red	あか・あかい	Have, There is (inanimate objects)	あります
Black	くろ・くろい	Have, There is (animate objects)	います
Blue	あお・あおい	To Do	します
Big	おおきい	To Go	いきます
Small	ちいさい	Understand	わかります
Top, Over	うえ	To Speak	はなします
Bottom, Under	した	To be, "is"	です

MY NOTES:

Lesson 2 Grammar : Particles and Basic Sentence Structure

The particles, か、に、は、と、も、が、の、へ、を are the foundation of the Japanese language. A good understanding of them now will save you time and confusion later!

は – TOPIC

This は is pronounced "wa" when used as a particle. It distinguishes a topic. This may or may not be the subject of a sentence.

Transform from English:

The bag is red.

➔The かばん is あかい。

➔かばんはあかい

➔かばんはあかいです。

Right away, Japanese let's us know the topic of the sentence. Note that は did not replace 'is' which was replaced with です. It is common in Japanese to distinguish the topic of the sentence first. Here's some more examples:

The desk is small	つくえはちいさいです。
The pencil is on the chair	えんぴつはいすのうえにあります。
Excuse me, is this the hospital	すみません。ここはびょういんですか。(ここ = here)

You Try: Create two sentences that use は and the vocabulary from Lesson two.

LESSON 2 GRAMMAR : PARTICLES AND BASIC SENTENCE STRUCTURE

に – DIRECTOR

に can be thought of as the equivalent to the English, "in," and can also direct action, indicating the time of action as well as the location of existence. Example: おかあさんはどこにいますか？

Transform from English:

Where are you?

→ どこ are you？

→ どこ are あなた？

→ あなたはどこにいますか？

The particle に is nicknamed the director because it directs action.

Where is the pen?	ぺんはどこにありますか？
Where should we go?	どこにいきますか？
I'm in Tokyo.	わたしはとうきょうにいます。

You Try: Create two sentences that use に and the vocabulary from Lesson two.

ANSWER THE QUESTION:

1) つくえはなにいろですか。What color is the desk?

____

2) いすはどこですか。Where is the chair?

____

3) へやはおおきですか。Is the room big?

____

Practice Numbers: **(**すうじのれんしゅう**)**

ひゃく	にひゃく	300	よんひゃく
ごひゃく	600	きゅうひゃく	700
せんひゃく	74	550	1,300

Create a Manga conversation of your own:

LESSON 3: VOCABULARY (TRAVEL PART 1)

	Japanese (日本語)	*Anime (アニメ)*
This way	こっち・こちら	こっち・こちら
That way (close to us)	そっち・そちら	そっち・そちら
That way (separated)	あっち・あちら	あっち・あちら
Which Way?	どっち・どちら	どれ
Sucks (no good)	いや	さいてい
Store	みせ	
Department Store	でぱーと	
Home	うち	
(Train) Station	えき	
Hotel	ほてる	
Restrooms	おてあらい・といれ	
Phone – Cell Phone	でんわ・けいたいでんわ	けーたい
Bus Stop	ばすてい	
Bank	ぎんこう	
Subway	ちかてつ	
Person	ひと	
Boy	おとこのこ	
Girl	おんなのこ	
Wife	おくさん	
Husband	ごしゅじん	
Food	たべもの	
Who?	だれ	
Here – There – There (separated)	ここ・そこ・あそこ	
Next to…	となり	
Close	ちかい	
Far	とおい	
How Much?	いくら？	なんぼ？

MY NOTES:

LESSON 3 GRAMMAR : PARTICLES AND BASIC SENTENCE STRUCTURE

が – CONTROLLER

Used for the subject of the sentence that is controlling something or doing something. A noun followed by が indicates the subject of a sentence while a noun followed by に indicates location.

Transform from English:

What is there?

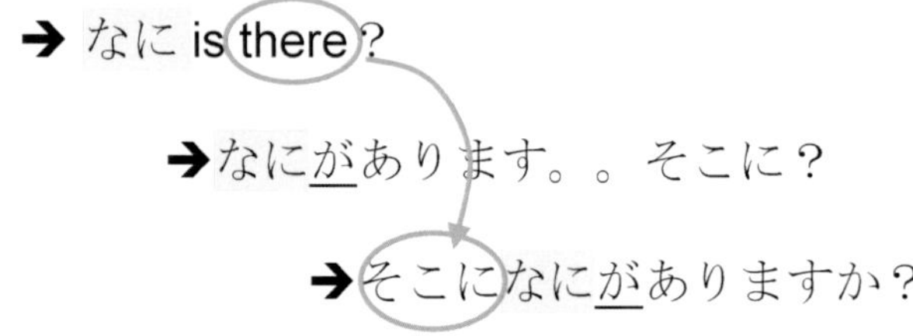

What is the difference between the particle は and the particle が？Think of は as the topic of a sentence while が is the subject. が connects the subject with the verb. It is nicknamed the controller because it controls who does what. If everyone in the conversation is already familiar with the topic (は), it is often dropped from the sentence; however, the subject is rarely dropped.

Here's some more examples:

There is a school in Tokyo	とうきょうにがっこうがあります
There is a department store in Osaka	おおさかにでぱーとがあります。
Who will speak?	だれがはなしますか？

か – QUESTION

In the last lesson you saw a sentence that ended with か. Adding か to the end of a sentence or partial sentence denotes a question. Example: いまはなんじですか。

Transform from English:
Who are you?

➔ だれ are あなた？

あなたはだれですか。

Will you come to my party?

➔（あなたは）　わたしのパーティーにきますか？

Note: In Japanese, the ? at the end of a question is optional.

NOTE:
We put あなたは in parenthesis since this can be dropped if we already know to whom we are referring.
JR せんせい

Grammar Points: *あります・います*

あります is used to express the existence of things which do not move by themselves.

います is used to express the existence of human beings and animals.

ほんがあります。	There is a book.
くろいぺんがあります。	There is a black pen.
わたしがいます。	I am here.
おくさんがいます。	(he) has a wife.

LESSON 3 GRAMMAR : これ、それ、あれ

これ、それ、あれ replace the English "this" and "that." In Japanese there are three demonstratives instead of two, giving more detail as to the position of an item:

これーUsed when the object is close to the speaker
それーUsed when the object is closer to the person being spoken to
あれーUsed when the object is neither close to the speaker nor the person to which he/she is speaking.
どれーMeans "Which one?"

Examples:

What is this? That is a dictionary.
これはなんですか。それはじしょです。
What is that? This is an umbrella
それはなんですか。これはかさです。
Is that a library? No, that is a hospital.
あれはとしょかんですか。いいえ、あれはびょういんです。

こっち、そっち、あっち

Similarly, こっち、そっち、あっち（Also, こちら、そちら、あちら）replace "this way," and "that way."

こっちーThis way, used when the path is close to the speaker
そっちーThat way, used when the path is closer to the person being spoken to
あっちーThat way, used when the path is neither close to the speaker nor the person to which he/she is speaking.
どっち,どちらー "Which way?"

Examples:

ほてるはどちらですか？　ほてるはこちらです。

ばすていはどちらですか？　あちらです。

えきはちかいですか？　はい、そちらです。

LESSON 3 PRACTICE (GETTING AROUND)

Translate to Japanese:

1) What is that? That is a Cell Phone.
2) Which way is the restroom? The restroom is this way.
3) Is that Tokyo subway? No, that's Shinawawa.
4) Who is that? That is my husband?

Usage(えん = Yen, Japanese currency)

Example using かばん

Mr. たなか：これはいくらですか。
Ms.いずみ：どれですか。
Mr.たなか：このかばんです。
Ms.いずみ：それはごせんえんです。

Repeat with these:

ほん

かさ

つくえ

とけい

Practice います(living)、あります(non-living)、です(is):

1）それはなんですか？　ぺん________

2）そちらにえきが_________

3）おんなのこが_________

4）ちかてつはちかい_______か？

5）おくさんはおてあらいに_________

CREATE A MANGA CONVERSATION

LESSON 4: VOCABULARY

	Japanese (日本語)	Anime (アニメ)
(I) Want	ほしい	
Thing or reference to	こと	
Crush (I like…)	すきです	(Adjective is すきな)
Study	べんきょう	
Student	せいと	
Teacher	せんせい	
College	だいがく	
Library	としょかん	
Toilet	といれ	
Post Office	ゆうびんきょく	
Shoes	くつ	
Coffee/Coffee Shop	こーひー	
Holiday	やすみ	
Weather	てんき	
Work; Job	しごと	
After That	そのあと	
Every Day	まいにち	
Every Night	まいばん	
Tonight	こんや	
Good	よい	
Bad	わるい	
Late; Slow	おそい	
Early; Fast	はやい	
Cold	さむい	
Hot	あつい	
Warm	あたたかい	
Love / To Love	あい	

Critical Verbs:

To go	いきます
To come	きます
To Study	べんきょうします
To Love	あいします

If you have time, learn the names of Months and Days in Appendic C.

MY NOTES:

LESSON 4 GRAMMAR : PARTICLES AND BASIC SENTENCE STRUCTURE

と – CONNECTOR

と is equivalent to the English "and." It's used to adjoin two or more nouns. It should not be used to join two non-related sentences.

Transform from English:

I like sushi and yakisoba.

➔I like sushi と yakisoba

➔すしとやきそばがすきです。

Kenji and Michael are here.

➔けんじさんとまいけるさんがいます。

I'll go to the department store and bank.

➔でぱーととぎんこうへいきます。

Note: there are no 'run on' sentences in Japanese, as long as proper grammer is followed, a sentence can go on forever (and some in technical papers actually do).

Create two sentences that use と and the vocabulary from Lesson 4:

へ – Mover

へ indicates the direction of movement with motion verbs. It is most commonly used with the verbs いく（いきます、to go） and くる（きます、to come）.

Transform from English:

I will go to the train station at 9:00 am.

➔ごぜんくじにえき will go

ごぜんくじにえきへいきます。

My mother will go to the post office.

➔おかあさんはゆうびんきょくへいきます。

(You try) The teacher will go to the library.

Create two sentences that use へ and the vocabulary from Lesson 4:

の – POSSESOR

There is no apostrophe s, (’s), in Japanese, rather, の is used in place of the “’s” or “of” as in “Michael’s umbrella” or “the umbrella of Michael.” It allows one noun to possess another.

Whose shoes are these?

➔このくつは(are) whose?

➔このくつはだれのくつですか？

Michael’s shoes：まいけるのくつです。

My name is . . . ：わたしのなまえは。。。

The front of the car is blue.

➔くるまのまえはあおいです。(まえ = front)

(You try) This hotel’s food is bad.

Create two sentences that use の and the vocabulary from Lesson 4:

LESSON 4 PRACTICE (DESCRIBE WHAT YOU MEAN)

Translate to Japanese

1) What is that? That's the teacher's bag.

____

2) Whose book it that? That is my wife's book.

____

3) Is the college far? No, the college is close.

____

4) I have a crush on Masao. (hint: Masao is the subject)

____

Translate these times: (If you need to, review lesson 1 at this time)

7:04 PM: ______________________________

11:57 AM: ______________________________

4:31 PM: ______________________________

12:48 AM: ______________________________

LESSON 5: VOCABULARY (FUN WORDS)

	Japanese (日本語)	*Anime (アニメ)*
Home	いえ	
Bald	はげ	
Yakuza	やくざ	
Foreigner	がいこくじん	がいじん
Therefore	だから	
Coffee	こーひー（コーヒー）	
When	いつ	
Bother; Bothersome	じゃま	
Umbrella	かさ	
Company	かいしゃ	
Computer	こんぴゅーた（コンピュータ）	
T.V.	てれび（テレビ）	
Mr. / Miss / Mrs.	さん	くん(boys) ちゃん(girls)
Person	ひと	
Man	おとこ	
Woman	おんな	
Bankrupt	とうさん	
Danger	あぶない	
Loud	うるさい	
Depressed	ゆううつ	
Quiet	しずかな	
Need	いります	いる
Become	（に）なります	
Touch	さわります	
To Do	する	
Drink	のみます	

MY NOTES:

____

____

____

____

____

____

____

____

____

____

____

For fun, the word ゆううつ uses very complex kanji:

憂鬱

Learn to write it and impress your Japanese friends!

LESSON 5 GRAMMAR : PARTICLES AND BASIC SENTENCE STRUCTURE

も – ALSO

も has the same function as the English "also" and "too" and it can replace the particles は、が、and を.

Transform from English

Kenji and Michael will also go.

➔けんじもまいけるもいきます。

I study at school. I also study at home.

➔がっこうでべんきょうします。いえでもべんきょうします。

（You Try）I have a T.V. I also have a computer.

Create two sentences that use も and the vocabulary from Lesson 5:

THIS ONE, THAT ONE . . . この、その、あの

この、その、あの are used the same as これ、それ、あれ; however, they always introduce a noun. For example, this pen: このぺん、that car: そのくるま.

Examples:

あのやくざはあぶないです。 That Yakuza is dangerous.

このおんなのひとはゆううつです。 This woman is depressed.

あのかさはごひゃくえんです。 That umbrella is 500 yen.

You try: Fill in the blank with これ、それ、あれ、この、その、あの、こっち、そっち、or あっち. (hint: these sentences make up one conversation)

1) ____________ ぺんはあなたのぺんですか？

2) ____________ ですか？

3) はい、____________ ぺんです。

4) ____________はぺんじゃありません。えんぴつです。

5) ああ、そうですか。ぺんはどこにありますか。

6) ぺんは____________のみせにあります。

7) ありがとう！

ENDING A SENTENCE: でしょう、ね、よ

でしょう replaces the verb です when the speaker wants to imply that it is his/her opinion, and not necessarily a fact. It can also be used by the speaker to invoke the opinion of the one being spoken to.

Examples:

That person is a Yakuza.
あのおとこのひとはやくざです。

Isn't that person a Yakuza?
あのおとこのひとはやくざでしょう。

Tomorrow's weather will be warm.
あしたのてんきはあたたかいです。

Don't you think tomorrow's weather will be warm?
あしたのてんきはあたたかいでしょう？

ね is added to the verb です and other verbs for emphasis. It can imply "isn't it…?," "isn't he/she…?," aren't they…?" It's often used to imply "I fully understand," as in そうですね。

That foreigner is vociferous.
➔あのがいじんはうるさいですね。

I get depressed when I go to school.
➔がっこうへいくとゆううつになりますね。

> The power of ですね :
> In the anime, Death Note, the character "N" uses ですね to indicate that even though the character "Lighto" also wants to catch the villian (Kira) there is some doubt as to his true intentions. Can you find this scene?

よ is added to the end of a sentence to emphasis a fact most often when the speaker feels that the person being spoken to needs the information or has a particular interest in a given situation. The speaker can use it to imply that he/she is teaching something to the person being spoken to.

That store is out of business. (said to a man trying to open the store's door)
➔あのみせはとうさんですよ。

(it's raining.) You'll need an umbrella
➔かさがいりますよ。

を – ACTION

を is the final fundamental particle that we will cover. We call it “Action” because it gives action (through verbs) to nouns.

Transform from English

I will drink coffee

➔I will drink コーヒー

コーヒーをのみます。（コーヒー　＝　こーひー）

I will buy a T.V.

てれびをかいます。

(You try) Tonight I will study Japanese.
I love Michael.

Create two sentences that use を and the vocabulary from Lesson 5:

Why are some words not written in Hiragana?
You may have noticed that some words are usually written with Katakana characters, like テレビ and コーヒー. Generally, words that are not native to Japanese are written in Katakana. Since we do not cover Katakana in this book, you may write them in Hiragana.

CREATE MANGA SCENES USING これ、それ、あれ、この、その、あの、でしょう、ね、よ。Feel free to use vocabulary not covered so far.

A note on で

で indicates the place where an action is performed. This was seen in the example set for も：いえでもべんきょうします。

Examples:

We drink coffee at the store. みせでコーヒーをのみます。

で can also indicate the means by which or with which an action is performed.
Examples:

I came by train
でんしゃできました。

Let's speak in Japanese
にほんごではなしましょう。

（You try） We will meet at the hospital.
Which way will you go?

Create two sentences that use で and the vocabulary from Lesson 5:

PRONUNCIATION PRACTICE(CONDUCT WITH YOUR INSTRUCTOR)

Practice the correct accent for these words:

1) びょういん　　Hospital
2) きょうしつ　　Classroom
3) しんじゅく　　Shinjuku (in Tokyo)
4) なかむら　　Mr. Nakamura
5) そうだん　　Consult
6) やくそく　　Promise
7) ばんごう　　Number
8) しゅうしょく　　Employment
9) しょり　　Process

JR's Advice
Practice the difference between しょ and しょう with your instructor. Include words that use this combination. Also pactice きょ and きょう。

More Practice:

1) たてもの　　Building
2) としょかん　　Library
3) ごしゅじん　　Husband
4) あかさか　　Akasaka (in Tokyo)
5) あおやま　　Aoyama (in Tokyo)

Practice the inclinations of ですね：

1) びょういんですね？(asking)
2) びょういんですね。(reply)

GENERAL PRACTICE FOR LESSONS 1 – 5

Translate into Japanese:

English:	Japanese:
The weather is warm. Therefore, I will take a holiday. I will go to Tokyo with Michael and Tanaka.	
Is Tokyo far?	
No, it's close.	
Will you go by train?	
No, we will go by car.	
What's in Tokyo?	
In Tokyo, there is a big department store.	
I will buy an umbrella and a bag.	
How much is the bag?	
It is 500 yen. (ですよ)	
What time will you leave? (leave = でます)	
I'll leave tonight at 5:30PM.	
Oh, that's late!	
Yes, I'll go now.	
Ok, Good-bye.	
Good-bye.	

CREATE A MANGA CONVERSATION

CONGRATULATIONS!
IN JUST 5 LESSONS, YOU CAN CARRY AN AVERAGE CONVERSATION IN JAPANESE.

LESSON 6: VOCABULARY (VERBS)

	Japanese (日本語) Anime (アニメ)
We	わたしたち
Supermarket	すーぱー（スーパー）
Apartment	あぱーと（アパート）
Elevator	えれべーた（エレベータ）
Tea	おちゃ
Water	みず
Always	いつも
Immediately	すぐ
Usually	たいてい
Sometimes	ときどき
Therefore	だから
A lot, Plenty, Many	たくさん
A Little (amount)	すこし
Fun, Upbeat	たのしい
Quiet	しずかな
Young	わかい
Green	みどり
To start	はじまります
To end	おわります
To read	よみます
To go back/return	かえります
To wake up	おきます
To Sleep	ねます
To see/look	みます
Sorry/Excuse me	しつれします (more serious than すみません)

MY NOTES:

Notice that some of these words are taken from English; hence, the use of Katakana.

LESSON 6 GRAMMAR : VERB CONJUGATION

In English we modify verbs to show present and past tense. The same is true in Japanese, only verbs are also modified to show level of politeness and respect. In fact, there are four official levels of politeness. For now, we'll concentrate on two: Plain form (also referred to as dictionary form) and polite form (also referred to as des – mas form). To find a verb in the dictionary, one must always use the plain form, hence, dictionary form. In this lesson we will learn this form.

So far we have presented verbs only in the des – mas form. When learning Japanese it is best to always use this form. Only switch to plain form when you become comfortable with the language and you're in the company of close friends.

First, you may have noticed that all of our examples so far are positive, that is, they indicate "I will. . . " What if you want to say, "I will not. . . "?

Negative VERBS

Verbs in negative form are created by turning ます into ません. です is replaced by じゃありません. You have already learned that to understand is わかります. Therefore, to not understand is わかりません.

Examples:

I will not go to the store. みせへいきません。

I will not drink coffee. コーヒーをのみません。

That is not a hospital. それはびょういんじゃありません。

Now, let's look at changing tense in Japanese. Future and present tenses are covered by the form ます and ません so you're already familiar with that tense. Let's look at past tense.

Past tense

Positive verbs are changed to past tense by replacing ます with ました.
Negative verbs are created by replacing ません with ませんでした.
です is replaced by でした.

Examples:

I went to the store	みせへいきました。
I didn't drink coffee.	コーヒーをのみませんでした。
That Yakuza was dangerous.	あのやくざはきけんでした。

Practice Present and Past tense

Sentence in Present Tense:	Sentence in Past Tense:
_いえにかえります________	______________________________
_いえにかえりません______	______________________________
_ろくじにねます__________	______________________________
_ろくじにねません________	______________________________
_すこしです______________	______________________________
_すこしじゃない__________	______________________________

CREATE A MANGA CONVERSATION USING ONLY NEGATIVE AND PAST TENSE VERB FORMS (TRY TO USE AN ENDING LIKE でしょう OR ですね). SOME HELPFUL VOCABULARY:

Morning = けさ, **Yesterday =** きのう, **Delicious =** おいしい, **Tastes bad =** まずい

THE PLAIN (FAMILIAR) FORM

The plain form is actually the basis for all other forms so next we'll learn the three types of plain forms. There are three categoris of verbs: う verbs, る verbs, and "Irregular verbs." There are only two irregular verbs, so you should concentrate on distinguishing between う and る verbs. This will take considerable thought initially, but as you practice with the instructor and friends and watch Anime or read Manga, you will soon be able to use the correct form without thinking.

う VERBS

We call these verbs, う verbs, because they end with the sound う. Note: we said, "sound," and not character. Words of this form end in う、く、ぐ、す、つ、ぬ、ぶ、む、る. The polite, des – mas, form of these verbs is formed by replacing the う sound with an い sound and adding ます.
Here are some examples:

かう　＝＝＞　かいます

いく　＝＝＞　いきます

よむ　＝＝＞　よみます

Why didn't we learn the plain from first?

Students are taught the polite form first since in Japanese, it is required to use the polite form when someone begins to converse in Japanese. Using the plain form when meeting someone for the first time is considered rude and should be avoided.

る VERBS

We call these verbs, る verbs, because they end with the character る. These verbs also precede る with the vowel い or え. The polite, des – mas, form of these verbs is formed by replacing the る with ます.
Here are some examples:

おきる　＝＝＞　おきます

ねる　＝＝＞　ねます

＊There are several verbs that follow this condition, but are conjugated as う verbs. This includes: かえる(return)、しゃべる(speak)、すべる(slip)、and more.

いる and いる

There is an う verb, いる, (いります = Need) and a る verb いる, (います = to exist, living thing).

IRREGULAR VERBS

The two irregular verbs are also the most used, namely, “to do” and “to come”:

する　＝＝＞　します

くる　＝＝＞　きます

する is indeed a special verb. You have noticed in lesson 4 that する can be added to nouns to transform them into verbs, as in べんきょう **=>** べんきょうする.

USING THE INTERNET OR A DICTIONARY, LOOK UP VERBS AND DECIDE THEIR FORM. FILL IN THE MISSING BLOCKS:

(Refer to Appendix B if you need help)

Dictionary, Plain form	Mas form	Negative Form	Past Form	Negative Past Form	What type of verb is this?
ある					
	ねます				
		おきません			
			いきました		
				よみませんでした	
	きます				
				しませんでした	
			はなしました		
		みません			
	かえります				
いただく					
	はじまります				
		べんきょうしません			
			すべりました		

USING THE PROPER VERB FORM IS VITAL TO SPEAKING JAPANESE SO LETS PRACTICE SOME MORE:

Answer the question in both the affirmative and negative form as shown:

Question:	Polite Form:	Anime: (Plain Form)
おきますか?	はい、おきます	うん、おきる
	いいえ、おきません	いや、おきない

ねますか?

かえりますか?

しますか?

のみますか?

みますか?

はじまりますか?

LESSON 7: VOCABULARY

	Japanese (日本語)	Anime (アニメ)
Cleaning/To Clean	そうじ・そうじする	
Breakfast-Lunch-Dinner	あさごはん・ひるごはん・よるごはん	
Novel	しょうせつ	
Magazine	ざっし	
Primary School	しょうがっこう	
Secondary School	ちゅうがっこう	
High School	こうこう	
Weekend	しゅうまつ	
Bath	おふろ	
Hungover	ふつかよい	
Tall / Short	せがたがい・せがひくい	
Often	よく	
Not often, not many	あんまり（+ない）	
How much?	どのぐらい	
Refrigerator	れいぞうこ	
Office	じむしょ	
To rain	（あめが）ふる	
To go out	でかける	
To know	しる	
To eat	たべる	
To search	しらべる	

MY NOTES:

Counters

As mentioned, Japanese has no apostrope s like English. Instead, a counter is placed after the number to indicate that an object or thing is plural. Each type of object has a different counter, for example, the counter used for sheets of paper, まい, is different from that used for bottles, ほん. As we saw with minutes, the pronunciation of the counter can change according to the number it's modifying. First, let's learn some of the 10 most used counters then we'll practice using those counters:

ほん	Long and cylindrical objects like trees and pens
まい	Flat, thin objects like paper, stamps, and dishes
こ	Small and compact objects This can also be used when you don't remember the correct counter
はい	Liquid in cups, bowls, and glasses
さつ	Bound objects like books and magazines, ex. Manga
だい	Machines including automobiles
かい	Building floors
けん	Buildings including houses
そく	Pairs of footwear including socks and shoes
つう	Letters and transmissions
ど	Times as in how many times it occurs

MORE ABOUT COUNTERS

The pronunciation of a counter changes according to the number for which it is being used. You surely noticed this in lesson one when you learned how to tell time. There, even though the counter for minutes is ふん、it became ぷん for the numbers 1, 3, 4, 6, 8, 9, and 10. Not all of the counters follow this rule, but several do. Below is an example. Also see Appendix D for more counters.

Review the counter for minutes:
いっぷん、にふん、さんぷん、よんぷん、ごふん、ろっぷん、ななふん、はっぷん、きゅうふん、じゅっぷん

Here are the counters for bottles and long objects:
いっぽん、にほん、さんぼん、よんほん、ごほん、ろっぽん、ななほん、はっぽん、きゅうほん

Note that some counters, for example ど and だい do not change per numeric value.

LETS PRACTICE USING COUNTERS

Translate to Japanese:

2 bottles ____________________

4 minutes ____________________

5 pieces of paper ____________________

7 books ____________________

3 buildings ____________________

The 8th Floor ____________________

3 cups of water ____________________

Stressed?
I know I was when I first learned counters which are a very different concept from English. Worry not; as you practice Japanese they become natural. ***JR***

MORE PRACTICE USING COUNTERS

Answer the question using the proper counters for the values 1,2,3,5,7, and 9:

1) ほんは、なんさつほしいですか？

2) いえまでなんぷんですか？(いえまで = Until we reach home)

3) れいぞうこにこかこら（Coke）はなんぼんありますか？

4) じむしょはなんかいですか？

5) ごはんはなんばいたべますか？(ごはん = rice)

"YET" . . . まだ AND "WELL" . . . もう

To express the notion, yet, as in "have not done yet," we use the term まだ. Put まだ in front of the negative present tense verb. For example, I will not go yet, まだいきません.
The term もう is used to express the feeling of "Well, I'll ~~ ," or "Well, I guess I'll ~~." For example, Well, I'm going now, もういきますよ.

Examples:
Will you clean your room? No, not yet.
へやのそうじをしますか？いいえ、まだしません。

Will you eat lunch now? No, I'm not going to eat yet.
もうひるごはんをたべませんか？いいえ、まだたべません。

Will you drink Sake today? Na, I'm hungover.
きょう、おさけをのみますか？いいえ、もうふつかよいです。

Anime Note: ***Why do Japanese say "もううううう" when they are mad?*** **It's common for Japanese to say もうううう when frustrated. This is an abreviation for もういいです。 Which means, "That's enough, or that's all I 'm going to take!"**

"MORE" . . . もっと

The Japanese word for more, もっと, sounds similar to the English more. Since there is no ~er, like in Bigger, もっと is simply placed before an adjective. It is similar to saying, "That is big. This is more big."

Examples:
Washington is a big city. Tokyo is bigger.
わしんとんはおおきいですね。とうきょうはもっとおおきいですよ。

The coffee shop is quiet. The library is even more quiet.
きっさてんはしずかです。としょかんはもっとしずかですよ。

"THE MOST" . . . いちばん

Japanese does not have a form of ~est, like biggest, or longest. To say that something is the most, the term いちばん (number one) is added. It's similar to saying, “”He is the number one fast runner.”

Examples:
Tokyo is a big city. Mexico city is the biggest city.
とうきょうはおおきなまちですね。めきしこしはいちばんおおきいまちですよ。

Tanaka san is tall. Well, John is the tallest.
たなかさんはせがたかいですね。もうじょんさんはいちばんせがたかいですよ。

"UNTIL" . . . まで

まで is used in two ways. First, it is used with time to express “until,” or “I will _ _ _ by _ _ _.”
Example:
I will return by 10 O'clock じゅうじまでにかえります。

It is also used say, unitil ___ happens, do ___.
Example:
Until I search him on the internet, I won't know his name. (いんたーねっと = internet)

いんたーねっとでしらべるまではなまえをしりませんでした。

*Notice that the plain form of the verb is used.

NOT VERY . . . あんまり（+ない）

To express the feeling of "not much" "not very" as in "…don't study very much" or "…didn't go very often" add あんまり before the negative form of the verb (present or past). Examples are あんまりべんきょうしない, and あんまりいかなかった.

Translate to Japanese:

1) My father is not very tall. (hint: not very tall = せがたかくありません)

____

2) I don't sleep very much.

____

3) I didn't read books a lot.

____

Create one sentence each using まだ、もう、もっと、いちばん

____

____

____

____

Translate to Japanese

1) That building is the tallest. It has 72 floors.

____

2) It's the most fun.

____

3) I have 13 Manga books in my house.

____

COMPLETE THE MANGA CONVERSATION

LESSON 8: VOCABULARY (ADJECTIVES/ADVERBS)

	Japanese (日本語)	Anime (アニメ)
English	えいご	
Japanese	日本語（にほんご）	
Green Pepper	ぴーまん	
Father	おとうさん	
Flag	はた	
Party	ぱーてぃー（パーティ	
Son	むすこ	
Movie Theatre	えいがかん	
Very (many)	とても	
Pretty	きれい	
Expensive	たかい	
Cheap	やすい	
New	あたらしい	
Old	ふるい	
Taste Good	おいしい	
Busy	いそがしい	
Healthy	げんきな	
Smell bad	くさい	
Soft	やわらかい	
Cute (boy)	かっこいい	
Cute (girl) or cute thing	かわいい	
Various	いろいろな	
To Meet	あう	
To Speak	はなす	
To be sufficient (have enough)	たりる	
To Use	つかう	

MY NOTES:

Grammar: Getting Familiar with the Familiar Form

It is fairly simple to form the plain negative forms of verbs (e.g. won't go, …didn't go), adjectives (e.g. not quiet), and nouns (e.g. not a book).

う Verbs

Plain Present Negative:	Replace the う sound with あ sound and add ない	かう => かわない いく => いかない よむ => よまない
Plain Past Negative:	Replace the う sound with あ sound and add なかった	かう => かわなかった いく => いかなかった よむ => よまなかった

る Verbs

Plain Present Negative:	Drop the ending る and add ない	おきる => おきない ねる => ねない
Plain Past Negative:	Drop the ending る and add なかった	おきる => おきなかった ねる => ねなかった

Irregular Verbs

する	しない	Plain Present Negative
	しなかった	Plain Past Negative
くる	こない	Plain Present Negative
	こなかった	Plain Past Negative

Nouns

Plain Present Negative:	Add じゃない to the end of the noun	ほてるじゃない くつじゃない
Plain Past Negative:	Add じゃなかった to the end of the noun	ほてるじゃなかった くつじゃなかった

You Try: Complete the following chart (Reference Appendix B if you get stuck)

		Plain Present Negative	Plain Past Negative
う Verbs	おわる		
	はじまる		
	のむ	のまない	
	ふる		ふらなかった
る Verbs	みる		
	たべる		たべなかった
	しらべる	しらべない	
	でかける		
Nouns	くるま		
	しょうせつ		

Translate to Japanese:

1) I don't drink coffee.

____

2) I didn't meet Miyuki.

____

3) I don't speak English.

____

4) That wasn't the Japanese flag.

____

5) That's not Masao's father.

____

Adjectives

There are two types of adjectives in Japanese, and they are easily distinguishable by the sound in which they end.

い　Adjectives end with the sound, "い" when they modify nouns.

な　Adjectives end with the sound, "な" when they modify nouns.

Examples:

My son bought a noisy car.

わたしのむすこはうるさいくるまをかいました。

(My son) has a beautiful bride.

きれいなおよめさんができました。

Notice **the use of できる. In Japanese we literally say "was able to get."**

There are various interesting movies at the theatre.

えいがかんにはいろいろなおもしろいえいががあります。

This is my small house.

これはわたしのちいさないえです。

Here an い adjective follows a な adjective. Also, we are using には to say "in" the theatre.

(You try) I have a very healthy dog.

____

(You try) Kenji has a cute girlfriend.

____

(You try) I bought a cheap computer.

____

THE PAST AND PRESENT FORM FOR ADJECTIVES

い adjectives and な adjectives form their ***affirmative past tense*** in different ways. For い adjectives, drop the い and add かった for the plain form and かったです for the polite form. For な adjectives, drop the な and add だった for the plain form and でした for the polite form. See the below table for Examples.

Negative forms are created using a similar format. For い adjectives, drop the い and add くない for the negative plain form and くありません for the negative polite form. The past negative plain form replaces the い with くなかった while the past negative polite form replaces the い with くありませんでした.
For な adjectives, drop the な and add じゃない for the negative plain form and じゃありません for the polite form. The past negative plain form replaces the な with じゃなかった while the past negative polite form replaces the な with じゃありませんでした.
See the below table for Examples.

	Present-Plain	Present-Polite	Past-Plain	Past-Polite
Affirmative	さむい (cold)	さむいです	さむかった	さむかったです
Negative	さむくない	さむくありません	さむくなかった	さむくありませんでした
Affirmative	きれいだ	きれいです	きれいだった	きれいでした
Negative	きれいじゃない	きれいじゃありません	きれいじゃなかった	きれいじゃありませんでした

Practice: Translate to Japanese. For each sentence, write the affirmative past tense (plain and polite), the present negative form(plain and polite), and the past negative form(plain and polite). The first one is done for you as an example.

1) His bride was/isn't/wasn't cute.

かれのはなよめはかわいかった。
かれのはなよめはかわいかったです。
かれのはなよめはかわいくない。
かれのはなよめはかわいくありません。
かれのはなよめはかわいくなかった。
かれのはなよめはかわいくありませんでした。

2) My car was/isn't/wasn't noisy.

____
____
____
____
____
____

3) That boy was/isn't/wasn't tall.

____
____
____
____
____
____

4) My house was/isn't/wasn't quiet.

____
____
____
____
____
____

5) The concert was/isn't/wasn't fun.

____
____
____
____
____
____

Joining Adjectives

Just as adjectives can appear as a series in English, so can they appear in Japanese. However, when conjoining adjectives, the ending of the first adjective is changed.
い Adjectives: Change the ending い to く and add て.
な Adjectives: Change the ending な to で.

Examples:
That car is new and fast.

あのくるまはあたらしくてはやいです。

My friend is quiet and smart.

わたしのともだちはしずかでかしこいです。

That actress (じょゆうさん) was young and beautiful. It's too bad she died.

あのじょゆうさんはわかくてきれいでした。しんでざんねんです。

*Note that the tense is decided by the last verb in the series.

Green peppers are green, sour, smelly, soft, and I hate them. (sour = すっぱい, hate = きらいな)

ぴーまんはみどり、すっぱくてくさくてやわらかくてきらいです。

*Note that the following is also acceptable for い adjectives:

おおきい、きれいなくるまです。

おおきくて、きれいなくるまです。

(You Try) My house is small, new, and quiet.

CREATING ADVERBS FROM ADJECTIVES

Adverbs are created by modifying adjectives in the following way:
い Adjectives: Change the ending い to く.
な Adjectives: Change the ending な to に.

Examples:
Please write clearly.

　　きれいにかきます。

I'll go quickly.

　　はやくいきます。

I got up late this morning.

　　けさ、おそくおきました。

I'll study quietly at the library.

　　としょかんでしずかにべんきょうします。

CREATE AN MANGA CONVERSATION USING ADJECTIVES AND ADVERBS

Adjective Clauses

Japanese does not use adjective clauses to describe nouns; rather, adjectives preceed nouns for description. This is known as a Noun Modifier. For example, instead of “The car, which is fast and red, belongs to Michael,” in Japanese we would say, “The fast red car belongs to Michael”: あのはやいあかいくるまはまいけるのくるまです。 The noun being described is underscored. Always us the plain form to modify a noun. Note these rules apply to adverb and verb clauses as well. Also, in the last example below, notice the use of の to separate nouns that modify another noun.

Examples:
The pepper that is green, sour, smelly, and soft, is trash.
　　あのみどりの、すっぱくて、くさくて、やわらかいぴーまんはごみです。

Mr. Tanaka will live in the house that was designed by Ms. Izumi
　　たなかさんはいずみさんがせっけいしたいえにすみます。

Mr. Lee, who is a Korean student, will live in Tokyo.
　　かんこくのがくせいのりーさんはとうきょうにすみます。

Practice Adjectives and Adverbs

Answer the question in Japanese:　(Use yes, はい, and no, いいえ, when needed)

1) えいがはながいですか？　(ながい = long)

____

2) せんせいはやさしかったですか？

____

3) にほんのはたはなにいろですか？（Hint: circle = まる）

____

4) あなたのともだちはどんなひとですか？

____

5) おとうさんはテレビをみますか？

____

Change the sentence so the adjectives modify the noun.

Example:

しごとはたいへんでした。
　　たいへんなしごとでした。

ほてるはしずかでした。

____

かのじょはきれいでした。

____

こどもはげんきでした。

____

がっこうはにぎやかでした。

____

えいがはおもしろくなかったです。

____

せんせいはひまでした。

____

Translate from English by turning the adjectives into adverbs:

Ex. I will talk loudly. うるさくはなす。

I will walk quickly. ____________________

I will speak in an upbeat way. ____________________

I will use it diligently. (diligently = ていねい) ____________________

LESSON 9: VOCABULARY (ACTION)

	Japanese (日本語)	*Anime (アニメ)*
And	そして	
Give me/Do for me	ください	
Please	おねがい	ちょうだい
House/Home	おたく(polite) いえ(house)	うち
Very Difficult	たいへん	
A Little	ちょっと	
Anytime	いつでも	
Again, In addition	また	
Boyfriend	かれ	
Girlfriend	かのじょ	
Electric	でんき	
Price	ねだん	
Wide	ひろい	
Narrow	せまい	
Problem	もんだい	
To Enter/ To go up/ To raise/To give	あげる・あがる	
To Wait	まつ	
To Listen	きく	
To Call	よぶ	
To Die	しぬ	
To Turn Off	けす	
To Stand	たつ	
To Sit	すわる	
To Open	あける	
To Close	しめる	
To break/Broken	こわれる	
To Fix	なおす	

MY NOTES:

ACTIONS IN PROGRESS . . . て form

Until now, we have only expressed actions that we are going to do or have already done. Next, we'll express verbs in their continuous form, like "reading," or "learning." This is refered to as the present participle in English. To do this, we convert the plain form of the verb to the て form and add いる. For the polite form, we convert the plain form of the verb to the て form and add います.
う verbs and る verbs convert to the て from in different manners as follows: (At this point you should review our earlier discuss on う and る verbs.)

For る verbs, simply drop る and add て+ いる(plain)・て+ います(polite)

おきる　==>　おきている、おきています
ねる　　==>　ねている、ねています

Usage:

おきていますか(Are you awake?). はい、おきています。
よしこさんはどこですか(Where is Yoshiko?). よしこさんはねている。

Converting う verbs to て form is a little more complicated, but you will quickly adopt:

If the verb ends in く、う、つ、る(verbs that end in る but are う verbs)

Drop the last character and add って+いる or って+います.
*We call っ the "small tsu" or ちいさい tsu. It actually represents "no sound" which is like a short pause in speech. English does not have such a pause, but some other languages do.

If the verb ends in む、ぬ、ぶ

Drop the last character and add んで+いる or んで+います.

If the verb ends in a "hardened" sound like ぐ

Drop the last character and add いで+いる or いで+います.
*Generally, we call the sound hardened when the tenten (``), is added, as ぐ is to く.

Finally, if the verb ends in す

Drop the last character and add している、しています.

Examples for う verbs

あう　＝＝＞　あっている (て form = あって + いる)
いく　＝＝＞　いっている
まつ　＝＝＞　まっている
とる　＝＝＞　とっている

よむ　＝＝＞　よんでいる
しぬ　＝＝＞　しんでいる
あそぶ　＝＝＞　あそんでいる

いそぐ　＝＝＞　いそいでいる

はなす　＝＝＞　はなしている

Converting irregular verbs to て form:

Change くる to きている or きています and する to している or しています.

*Notice how する is conjugated similar to う verbs ending in す.

Examples:

1) なにをしていますか？ほんをかいています。(To Write = かく)

2) エレベータでいきましょう。だめです、エレベータはこわれています。

3) でんきは？はい、けしています。

4) ごしゅじんはどこですか？いえでまっています。

PLAIN PAST AFFIRMATIVE

Now that we know the て form, we can form the plain past affirmative forms of verbs. Until now, we have used the です – ます form to do this, as in たべました。

る ***Verbs***, drop る and add た.

おきる　＝＝＞　おきた
ねる　＝＝＞　ねた

う ***Verbs***, convert to て form as previously explained; however, use た instead of て and だ instead of で

あう　＝＝＞　あった
いく　＝＝＞　いった
まつ　＝＝＞　まった
とる　＝＝＞　とった
よむ　＝＝＞　よんだ
しぬ　＝＝＞　しんだ
あそぶ　＝＝＞　あそんだ
いそぐ　＝＝＞　いそいだ
はなす　＝＝＞　はなした

Converting irregular verbs to plain past affirmative:

Change くる to きた and する to した.

PLAIN PAST PARTICIPLE AFFIRMATIVE

We can easily turn the above verbs to plain past participles, like "I was eating" by adding いた to the て form.
Examples:

ねる　＝＝＞　ねていた
あう　＝＝＞　あっていた
いく　＝＝＞　いっていた
よむ　＝＝＞　よんでいた
あそぶ　＝＝＞　あそんでいた
はなす　＝＝＞　はなしていた

PRACTICE WITH ACTIONS IN PROGRESS

You try, translate to Japanese into the plain form:

I'm writing a report. (Report = れぽーと)

____

I'm fixing the car.

____

My girlfriend/boyfriend is waiting.

____

Where was your father? He was eating.

____

You can turn the ている form into an adjective (noun modifier) by placing it in front of a noun.

Example:
Over there is a person using a cell phone.
あそこでけいたいをつかっているひとがいます.

You try:

Over there is a person drinking coffee.

____

Over there is a person eating lunch.

____

Here are children studying.

____

This is a broken car.

____

ASKING …ください

Now that you have mastered the て form, you can use it to make requests. To request that someone do something for you, add ください to the て form.

Example:
Please awake at 8 O'clock.
はちじにおきてください。

You try, translate to Japanese::
Please read this.

____

Please wait here.

____

Please call Hiroko.

____

*Mastering the て form is critical to using Japanese grammar fluently and understanding Anime. Take a few minutes to review the verbs in Appendix B. Practice converting to the て form without looking at the chart.

I THINK, I SAID …とおもいます…といいます

By now you want to say "I think" or "I said" in Japanese. This is easily accomplished by using the particle と and adding the verb for "to think, おもいます" or "to say, いいます," to the plain form of a sentence. To use the plain form of "to think," or "to say," simply conjugate their dictionary verbs, おもう, and いう, respectively, into the plain form.

Examples:
I think I'll leave at 7 O'clock.

しちじにでるとおもいます。

Aya said the price is expensive.

あやちゃんはねだんがたかいといいました。

You try, translate to Japanese:

I think I'll eat that.

____

I think the the building was red.

____

He said he would come.

____

She said she is studying piano.

____

When should I use the plain form?

At this point in your studies, you should use the polite form when speaking. However, it is imperative for you to be familiar with the plain form since you will hear this spoken in Anime and may be used when someone speaks to you. After you complete this book and develop close relationships with Japanese friends, you can begin to use the plain form.

CREATE AN ANIME CONVERSATION USING THE て FORM.

Some helpful vocabulary: Pet fish = さかな, **Alive =** いきる

PRONUNCIATION PRACTICE(CONDUCT WITH YOUR INSTRUCTOR)

Practice the correct accent for these names:

1) すずき
2) たなか
3) いとう
4) まえだ
5) よしだ
6) みしま

Ask your instructor to check your annunciation of the following sounds:
(Repeat faster & faster. Who is the fastest in your class?)

あ	い	う	え	お	お	わ	う	い	え
か	き	く	け	こ	う	お	い	え	あ
さ	し	す	せ	そ	く	こ	き	け	か
た	ち	つ	て	と	しょ	しょう	しよう		
な	に	ぬ	ね	の	きょ	きょう	きよう		
は	ひ	ふ	へ	ほ	ひ	ひょう	みょう		
ま	み	む	め	も	お	も	み	め	ま
や	い	ゆ	え	よ	る	ろ	り	れ	ら
ら	り	る	れ	ろ	り	りょ	りょう		
わ	い	う	え	お	こ	ご	ほ	ぼ	ヴ

Practice the following vocabulary with your instructor:

よみました
とうろく
しょうゆ
やりました
しょくどう

としょかん
しゅうしょく
ゆうびん
かいています
しょしょ (not a word)

LESSON 10: VOCABULARY

	Japanese (日本語)	*Anime (アニメ)*
Japanese	にほんご　（日本語）	
Spanish	すぺいんご	
Chinese	ちゅうこくご	
Phone Number	でんわばんごう	
Business Card	めいし	
History	れきし	
Clothes	ふく・ようふく	
Young Brother	おとうと	
Older Brother	おにいさん	
Younger Sister	いもうと	
Older Sister	おねえさん	
Grandmother	おばあさん	
Grandfather	おじいさん	
Detailed	こまかい	
Late	あとで	
Long Ago	むかし	
Chubby Girl	（お）でぶちゃん	
What's Wrong?	どうした	
To Have	もつ	
To Sell	うる	
To Write (or To Paint)	かく	
To Cut Class	さぼる	
To Work (for)	（に）つとめる	
To Throw Away (trash)	すてる	
To Learn	ならう	
To Drive	うんてんする	
Grades	せいせき	

MY NOTES:

Grammar: Using a sentence as a noun modifier. When to use が and の

In lesson 8 we discussed how adjective clauses are handled in Japanese. Here we see that the noun modifier can be an entire sentence. The subject of this type of sentence is indicated by が. の is also occasionally used; however, since が is always correct, we suggest students use が initially and の when they advance to the next level.

Examples:

わたし<u>が/の</u>うんてんするくるまはとよたです。

まさおくんはぼく<u>が</u>すてたたべものをたべました。

あなた<u>が</u>くれたぺんはかけません。

You try: Translate to Japanese

1) Please call that person over there who is waiting for the train.

____

2) Isn't that chubby girl who is eating sushi Miki's younger brother?

____

3) My younger brother ate the rice that I threw away yesterday.

____

MORE USES FOR と

We've seen how と can be used to join nouns and to add "I said," and "I think." Now we see how と can be used to express the notion of "together with" in English. Note the use of て form in the following sentences.

ぼくはせんせいとはなしてもんだいがわかりました。
I talked with the teacher and understood the problem.

きのうまいけるくんとみせへいってたべものをかいました。
Yesterday, I went to the store with Michael and bought some food.

You try, translate to Japanese:
I went with my younger brother to the store and bought a book on Chinese.

____

PRACTICE WITH PLAIN FORMS

Convert the following vocabulary to plain form.
Examples:
ひま：

ひまです	ひまだ
ひまでした	ひまだった
ひまじゃありませんでした	ひまじゃなかった

1) やましたさん

2) しずか

3) そう

Use the plain form as a modifier

Example: けさしんぶんをよみました

けさよんだしんぶん

1) さきみせにはいりました

____

2) このあいだおばあさんとはなしました

____

3) まちでじこをみました (じこ = Accident)

____

4) きのうえいがをみました

____

5) おおさかでびでおをとりました

____

Convert the active verb to a passive verb by using a noun modifier

Example: わたしはごはんをつくりました。

わたしがつくったごはん

1) わたしたちはしょくどうにはいりました。

____

2) ぼくはえいがをみました。

____

3) ぼくはにほんごをならいました。

____

Expand on this: add これは and とちがいます to the phrases you made above.
Example:
これはけさよんだしんぶんとちがいます。

____

____

____

____

____

____

____

____

Translate the following to your instructor orally:

What's wrong?
There's no dictionary.
Is that right? Isn't it this one?
No, that's different than the dictionary I was using.
Is that right. Oh, there it is, on top of the chair.
Ah, thank you.

What's wrong?
There's no wallet.
Is that right? Isn't it this one?
No, that's different than my wallet.
Is that right. Oh, there it is, on the floor.
Ah, thank you.

You had better/You should. . . ほうがいい

Expressing "You had better," or "You should" as in "You should go early" is accomplished by adding ほうがいい to the plain past form for an affirmative action (You had better . . .) and adding ほうがいい to the plain negative present form for a negative action (You had better not . . .)

Examples:
It will rain. You had better go by bus.
あめがふります。ばすでいったほうがいいですよ。

This milk is bad. You should not drink it. (milk = ぎゅうにゅう)
このぎゅうにゅうはだめです。のまないほうがいいです。

Your grades suck. You better study more.
きみのせいせきはだめです。もっとべんきょうしたほうがいい。

You try, translate to Japanese:
That umbrella is broken. You should throw it away.

____

Change a verb into a noun

Verbs are changed into nouns by adding の to their plain form and following with は or が.

Examples:
Learning Japanese is fun!
にほんごをべんきょうするのはたのしいです。

It's difficult to write a book.
ほんをかくのはむずかしいです。

My hobbie is watching Anime. (しゅみ = hobby)
あにめをみるのはわたしのしゅみです。

You try: Convert the verb in the phrase on the left into a noun and match with an adjective on the right.

てれびをみる	たのしいです
ようふくをかう	たいへんです
すぺいんごをならう	おいしいです
おおさかのたべものをたべる	おもしろいです

1) ______________________________

2) ______________________________

3) ______________________________

4) ______________________________

CREATE AN MANGA CONVERSATION BETWEEN A TEACHER AND STUDENT USING THE GRAMMAR POINTS OF LESSON 10

(teacher uses plain form, student uses polite form)

LESSON 11: VOCABULARY

	Japanese (日本語)	*Anime (アニメ)*
Gift	おみやげ	
They	かれら	
How old (age)	いくつ	
Senior (higher ranking)	せんぱい	
Candy	おかし	
Reputation	ひょうばん	
Popular	にんき	
Tonight	こんばん / こんや	
Shirt/s	しゃつ	
President	だいとうりょう	
Engineer	ぎし	
Very	ずいぶん	
Famous	ゆうめい	
The Other Day	このあいだ	
Worry	しんぱい	
Other (noun)	べつの	
For Sure	たしかに	
Math	すうがく	
Dorky / Uncool	ださい	きもい
To Get Thin	やせる	
To Get Fat	ふとる	
To Know	しる	
Can Do it	できる	
To Show	みせる	
Take (a photo)	（しゃしんを）とる	
Enter (a room)	はいる	

MY NOTES:

Can I . . .

The potential form, “Can I . . .,” or “I can . . .” used to express the notion of “I am able to” or “It is possible . . .” is employed by conjugating each verb form as noted below. This is not the form to use when asking permission which will be covered later.
*Note that once converted, all verbs in the potential form are る verbs.

う Verbs: Change the ending う sound to える
Examples:

かう ——> かえる I can buy
かく ——> かける I can write
はなす ——> はなせる I can speak
よむ ——> よめる I can read
まつ ——> まてる I can wait
かえる ——> かえれる I can return
あそぶ ——> あそべる I can play

る Verbs: Change the ending る to られる
Examples:

やめる ——> やめられる I can stop/quit
おきる ——> おきられる I can wake up

Irregular Verbs:

くる ——> これる I can come
する ——> できる I can do …

Convert the following verbs into the potential form:

あるく	Walk	あるける	あるけない
のる	Ride		
のむ	Drink		
つかう	Use		
みせる	Show		
よぶ	Call		

WHILE. . . ながら

To show that two actions are taking place simultaneously, add ながら to the verb root of one of the actions. To derive a verb's root, use the ます form, but drop the ます.

Some examples of verb roots:

します	＝＝＞	し
まちます	＝＝＞	まち
おきます	＝＝＞	おき

Example (use ながら):
うんてんをします。
でんわをします。
＝＝＞うんてんをしながらでんわします。

You try: (Translate and combine using ながら)

1) I watch TV.
   I eat dinner.

2) I ride the train.
   I use my cell phone.

3) I watch the movie.
   I talk to my friends.

4) I listen to the teacher.
   I dream of becoming a ….. (fill in with your dreams)

If . . . (え) ば

The notion of “if” is expressed by conjugating the verb to end in the え sound and adding ば. This is very similar to the conjugations for the potential form.

う Verbs: Change the ending う sound to え sound plus ば

Examples:

かう ——> かえば

かく ——> かけば

はなす ——> はなせば

よむ ——> よめば

まつ ——> まてば

かえる ——> かえれば

あそぶ ——> あそべば

る Verbs: Change the ending る to られば

Examples:

やめる ——> やめれば

おきる ——> おきれば

Irregular Verbs:

くる ——> くれば

する ——> すれば

Examples

1) ほんをかけばたくさんうれるかもしれません。

2) がっこうをさぼればせいせきがわるくなりますよ。

3) おんなのこがやせればおとこのこにんきがでますよ。

MAYBE. . . かもしれません

The notion of "Maybe . . .," and "Potentially. . .," is easily expressed by adding かもしれません (polite) and かもしれない (plain) to the plain form of a verb. This works for adjectives as well; however, for な adjectives, drop だ.

Example:
こんやのえいがにいきますか？
　　ええ、いくかもしれません。

おおさかはとおいでしょう？
　　うん、そうですね。とおいかもしれない。

IT'S BEST THAT . . .いいんです

Often, えば, is followed by いいんです. This expresses the concept, "You should. . ." or "It's best that. . ."　Use いいんです for the polite form and いいんだ for the plain form.

Examples:
たばこをやめればいいんです。

ここはどこですか。しりませんね。あのひとにきけばいいんだ！

うごきませんね。くるまをなおせばいいんだ。とりあえず、ここにおいたままでいいんです。(とりあえず = For now, おく = set (here), leave (here), まま = as it is)

I EXPECT . . . はずです

By now, you've seen that Japanese grammar often expresses concepts by adding syllables to the plain form of the verb. Expressing the notion that something is expected is no different. To say, "I expect. . .," "It's expected that . . .," or "It is supposed to . . ." simply add はず to the plain form verb, い adjective, な adjective (include な) or のはず to nouns. To form the negative, add はずはない (plain form) and はずはありません (polite form).

Examples

らいねんあめりかにいきますか？ええ、いくはずです。(う Verb)(らいねん = next year)

ぎしはすうがくがわかっているはずです。(て from Verb)

たなかさんはおさけをのむはずはない。(う Verb)

あきたのおんなのこはきれいなはずです。(な Adjective)(あきた = Akita Prefecture)

SAID . . . って

We saw in Lesson 2 that と is used to say, "I think" and "I said." A more informal way of expressing this same concept is to simply add って to the end of a sentence. This is often used when saying, "He said that . . . " This form is used very often in Anime.

Polite Form	Anime (informal)
いしかわさんもいくといいました。	いしかわさんもいくって
せんせいはわたしのせいせきがだめだといいました。	おれのせいせきがだめだって
おかねがないといっていました。	かねがないといったって

PRACTICE, "CAN YOU. . ."

Translate the following into Japanese

1) Can you read a Japanese Dictionary?

   ____

2) Can you write in Japanese?

   ____

3) Can you fix my car?

   ____

PRACTICE, "IF. . .えば"
"MAYBE. . .かもしれない"

Translate the following into Japanese

1) If you wake up at 6am, you will get a gift.

   ____

2) If you call her, she may go to the movie.

   ____

3) If you eat that candy, you'll get fat.

   ____

Answer the following using かもしれない、

1) ぼくのくるまははやいでしょう。

____

2) たなかさんはいそがしい？

____

3) あのしゃつはうりきれました？

____

4) わたしもだいとうりょうになれますか？

____

Practice える(can do)、ながら、かもしれません

Translate to Japanese:

1) Can they speak Japanese?

____

2) Is that person our Senior? Yes, he/she is possible our Senior.

____

3) I can call America on my cell phone.

____

4) Maybe I can learn history while riding the bus.

____

LESSON 12: VOCABULARY

	Japanese (日本語)	*Anime (アニメ)*
Search	けんさく	
Google	ぐーぐる	
Joke	じょうだん	
Country	くに	
Long Time-No See	ひさしぶり	
Birthday	おたんじょうび	たんじょうび
Painful	いたい	いったー
Much,all the way,by far	ずっと	
Very Nice	りっぱな	
Skillful	じょうず	
Not Skillful	へた	
Sufficiently	じゅうぶん	
To Dry	かわく	
To Search	さがす	
To Smoke	すう	
To Forgive	ゆるす	
To Get Crowded	こむ	
To Empty Out	すく	
Catch a Cold	かぜをひく	
Confused/Troubled	こまる	
Get Tired	つかれる	
To Park (a car)	ちゅうしゃする	
Cut hair (geta hair cut)	(かみを)きる	
To Calculate	けいさんする	
Attend Class (or meeting)	しゅっせき	

MY NOTES:

GIVING AND RECEIVING . . . あげるーくれる

Where English uses grammar to dictate the direction in which tangible and non-tangible objects are exchanged, ex. I give you, You give me, in Japanese, the direction in which objects are exchanged is indicated by vocabulary: あげる used for "I give you." and くれる for "You give me."
When you do something for someone or they do something for you, add あげる(you do for them) or くれる(they do for you) to the て form of the verb (action being done).

Example when you give something to someone else:
えんぴつをあげます。 I'll give you this pencil.

このほんをあげる。 I'll give you this book.

Example when you do something for someone else:
えんぴつをかしてあげます。 I'll lend this pencil to you.

このほんをかってあげます。 I'll buy this book for you.

Example when you receive something from someone else:
えんぴつをくれます。 Give me the pencil.

このほんをくれる? Will you give me this book?

Example when someone does something for you:
えんぴつをかしてくれますか? Will you lend this pencil to me?

このほんをかってくれる? Will you buy this book for me?

Why don't we need to use I, me, or you?

By using separate words to indicate the direction of giving, Japanese can leave out the I, me, or you since it is easily implied. The I, me, and you is easily added to these sentences by adding わたしはあなたに.... をあげる。

Simple? Wait, there's more. Because Japanese is a language that incorporates different levels of politeness and the act of giving and receiving connects different levels of politeness, the terms used to express give and receive change according to who you are talking to.

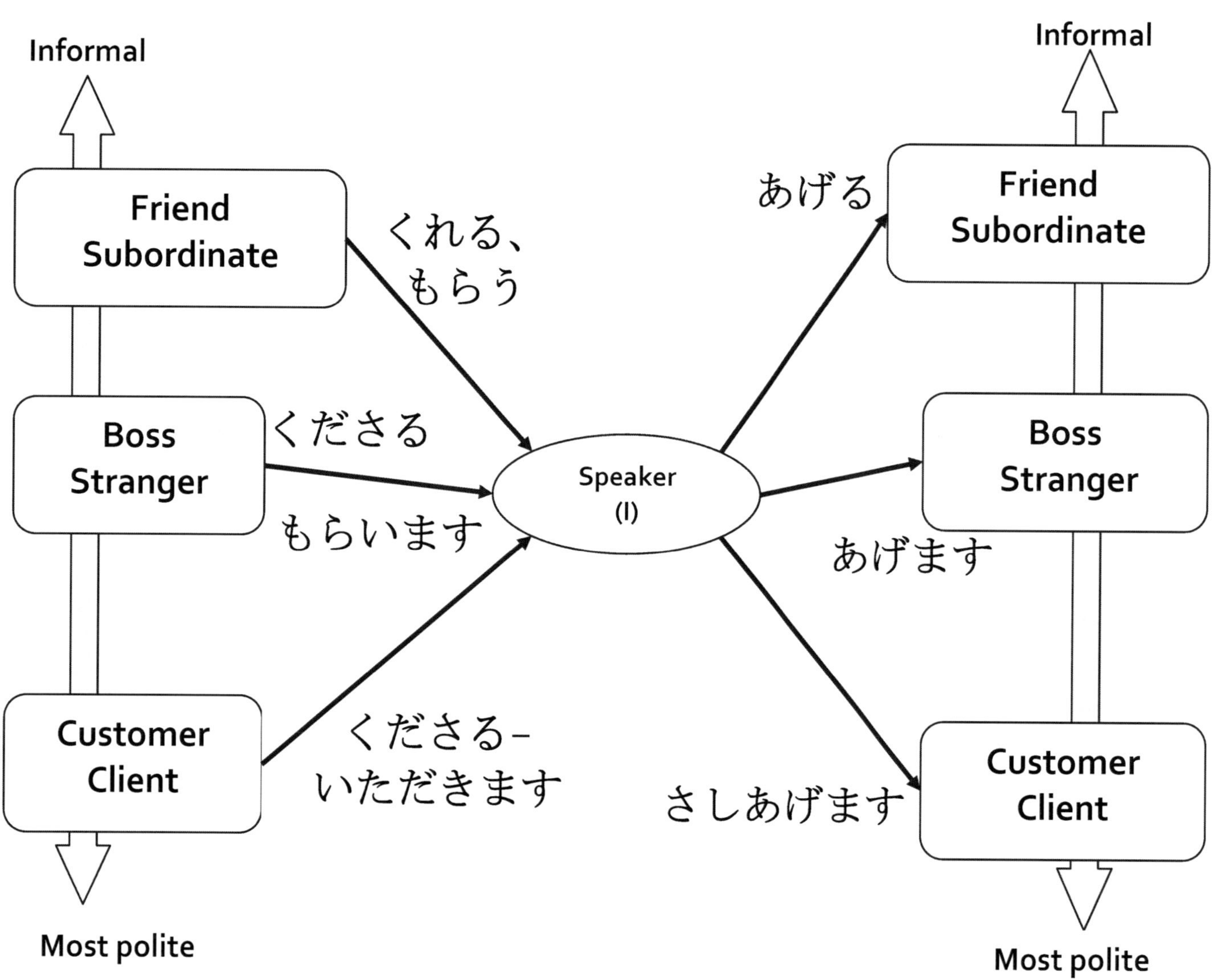

When describing objects or actions given between two people, use the form that matches the relationship of those two people. For example, if a student gives something to a teacher, use the polite form, あげます, rather than the informal, あげる. If the two parties are at an equal level, use あげる.

Examples:
Masao gave it to our teacher.
まさおくんがせんせいにあげました。

Our teacher gave it to me.
せんせいはぼくにほんをくれた。

Takanaka gave the dictionary to Masao.
たなかさんはまさおくんにじしょをあげた。

Write the Japanese that best describes the situation.
Example:
Your friend gave you one dollar.
ともだちがいちドルをくれた。

1) Your older brother gave you a car. (hint: older brother is at a higher level than you)

____

2) A stranger (unknown person) gave your younger sister some chocolate. (chocolate = ちょこれーと)

____

3) You ask your friend, “Did Tanaka san give you something for your birthday?”

____

4) Your friend, Ishikawa, gave his girlfriend some flowers.

____

PRACTIVE GIVING AND RECEIVING

Translate the following to Japanese:

(to your boss) I'll give you a copy of this report.

____

(to your friend) I'll give you a ride to high school.

____

(to your boss) I'll do it for you.

____

(asking your friend) Yes, do that for me.

____

(asking your teacher) Yes, will you talk to Ms. Izumi for me?

____

(asking your mother) Will you cut my hair?

____

(to your teacher) I will calculate it for you.

____

(before each meal, "you honorably receive this meal")

____

(to your boyfriend/girlfriend) Come over here now.

____

REQUESTING . . . ていただけますか

We've seen that we can ask for something (Please . . .) by adding ください to the て form. Similar to giving and receiving, a request should match the appropriate level of politeness. Actually, ください is only acceptable in informal speech. When you speak to a teacher, customer, or someone older, use the polite form. The chart below shows the many choices available. All of the words in the chart have the same meaning as ください.

あしたはやくおこして. . .

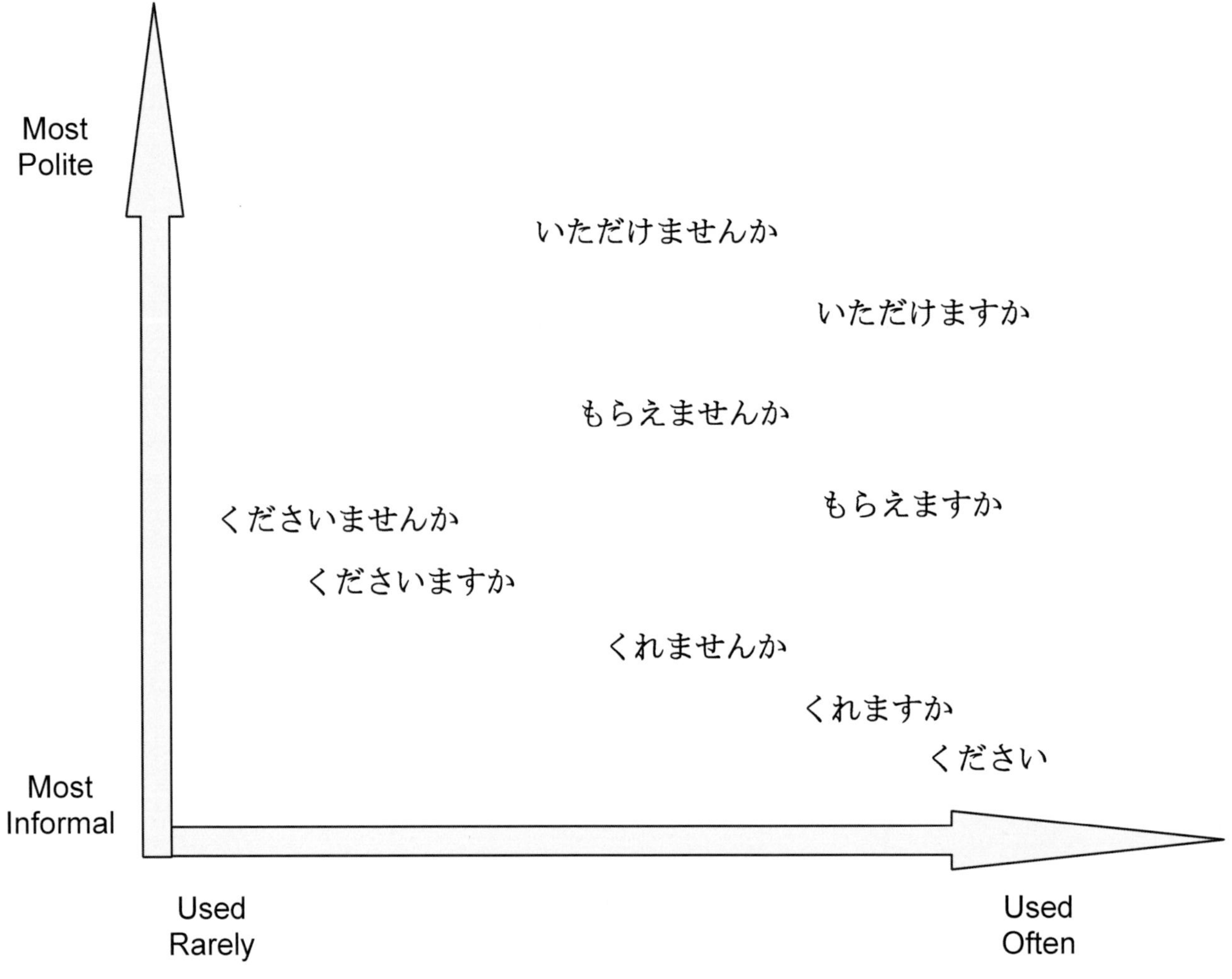

*The verbs here are shown as a question. The same structure applies to past, present, negative forms.

For informal situations only, it's also possible to simply use the て from of the verb. Note that this form should be used with care as it may be conceived as an order.

Examples:
Ask the teacher. せんせいにきいて

Go next door. となりにいって

Match the correct form of receive with the sentence (hint: all sentences will use the past form) (しょうかい = introduce)

まいけるくんがほんをかして________________________________。

せんせいにおもしろいことばをおしえて____________________________。

ともだちにしゅくだいをてつだって_________________。

だいとうりょうからしょうかいをして_____________________。

I WANT . . . てほしい

If you want something to happen, as in, "I want _ _ _ to do _ _ _." Use the て from plus ほしい for informal speech, て form plus もらいたい to be more formal, and て form plus いただきたい to be most polite.

Example:
I want you to introduce him (to me). かれをしょうかいしてほしい。

Use the correct form of ほしい、もらいたい、いただきたい:

1) I want him to get well soon. (get well = げんきになる)

____

2) I want you to get my computer for me. (get = とる)

____

3) Teacher, I would like you to give a speech. (speech = すぴーち)

____

PERMISSION . . . てもかまいませんか

If you want to ask permission, use the て form and add もいいですか for informal speech and もかまいませんか for polite speech. Notice there is no word for "May" as in "May I . . ." Rather, in Japanese we say, "If I do this, is it okay?" That is, かまいませんか is similar to saying, "Do you mind if. . ."

Examples:

Can I smoke here?	たばこをすってもいいですか？
May I sit here? (to a stranger)	ここにすわってもかまいませんか？

You Try:

1) May I open the window? (window = まど)

____

2) Is it alright if I don't do my homework?

____

3) Can I park (this car) here?

____

4) President Matsumoto, may I attend this meeting?

____

TRY IT . . . てみる

Japanese has no word for "Try" as in "Lets try it." Instead, the verb, みる, is added to the て form of a verb to convey "Do it and see (what happens).

Example
I will try Japanese food.
にほんりょうりをたべてみる。

あなたもやってみてください：

I will try Sake.

____

I will go and check it out.

____

I will try asking her.

____

I will try fixing the car.

____

I will try writing a letter.

____

MUST . . . しないとだめ　しなくちゃ

There is no word for "Must" in Japanese. Rather, we say, "If _ _ _ doesn't happen, it is not good." Or "If it doesn't happen, it won't work." We can do this in three ways. First, we can add とだめ to the plain negative form of a sentence.

Example:

I must go. いかないとだめ (literally, If I don't go, it's bad)

The other way is to drop the い in negative plain form verbs and add ければならない. For "To Go" the conjugation would be: いかない (minus い) plus ければならない。 Therefore, I must go = いかなければならない (literally, if I don't go, it won't happen)

Examples:

I must walk. あるかなければならない

I must see. みなければならない

Finally, we can add なくてはならない (polite) or なくちゃ (informal) to the negative form of the verb after removing the final ない.

Here, "I must go" would be: いかない (minus ない) plus なくてはならない for いかなくてはならない. (as above, If I don't go, it won't happen)

Convert the verbs あげる、よむ、and いう to each of the forms for must:

. . . とだめ	ければならない	なくてはならない・なくちゃ

CREATE AN MANGA CONVERSATION BASED ON LESSON 12

Use the following scenario with the vocabulary and grammar of lesson 12 to form a story.

Story Synopsis: Kenji asks his little sister, Aya, to help him bake a cake for Hiroko's birthday. She says Ok, but wants him to buy the ingredients. He doesn't have a car so he asks if he can use her car.

Helpful vocabulary: Cake = けーき, ingredients = ざいりょう, be careful = きをつける

LESSON 12 GENERAL PRACTICE

Make the following requests in Japanese:

1) Sensei, may I leave early today?

____

2) Can I use the restroom?

____

3) May I ride along?

____

Tell them what you want (hint, use てほしい)

1) Please turn the radio off.

____

2) Please search on the internet.

____

3) Please let me stay here tonight.

____

Tell them what you must do

1) I must call my mother.

____

2) I must exercise more.

____

3) I must make that train.

____

REVIEW EVERYTHING COVERED IN BOOK 1

For the next three pages, complete the Manga conversation using the grammar you have learned in this book.
Story Part 1: Masao and Miyuki notice Michael, who is a new student that just arrived from America. Hiroko introduces herself. Michael wants to use her phone. Hiroko thinks that it's to call America, but he wants to call his homestay family.

Story Part 2: Michael, Masao, Miyuki, and Hiroko go to see the cherry blossoms (さくら) together. Hiroko notes the beauty of the sakura trees. Michael tells them that sakura trees also exist in America. Miyuki asks Masao to take her picture with Michael.

Story Part 3: Kenji, Miyuki, Aya, and Michael must take a test the next day. Michael needs to study all night to prepare for the test; however, he thinks he'll be too tired to take the test if he studies all night. Kenji offers to make a practice test for him. Michael asks Miyuki to check his answers, but she tells him to ask Aya. Aya is not happy about Miyuki's comment.

Appendix A: Practice Test 1 for Hiragana

Fill in the hiragana for the romanji letters listed below:

A ____________

I ____________

E ____________

O ____________

U ____________

KA ____________

TA ____________

HA ____________

NA ____________

SA ____________

BA ____________

HE ____________

HO ____________

KE ____________

KI ____________

KU ____________

SHI ____________

SU ____________

SE ____________

SO ____________

TSU ____________

TE ____________

TO ____________

HU/FU ____________

MA ____________

MI ____________

MO ____________

NI ____________

NO ____________

YA ____________

YU ____________

WO ____________

HYO ____________

KYO ____________

SHO ____________

MYO ____________

CHU ____________

CHO ____________

SHU ____________

Appendix B: Verb Conjugation Chart

Dictionary Form	ーます Form	ーて Form	Past	Negative Present	Potential	ば Form	ーたら Form	Volitional	Imperative
いる	います	いて	いた	いない	いられる	いれば	いたら	いよう	いろ
借りる	かります	かりて	かりた	かりない	かりられる	かりれば	かりたら	かりよう	かりろ
食べる	たべます	たべて	たべた	たべない	たべられる	たべれば	たべたら	たべよう	たべろ
やめる	やめます	やめて	やめた	やめない	やめられる	やめれば	やめたら	やめよう	やめろ
会う	あいます	あって	あった	あわない	あえる	あえば	あったら	あおう	あえ
泣く	なきます	ないて	ないた	なかない	なける	なけば	ないたら	なこう	なけ
行く	いきます	いって	いった	いかない	いける	いけば	いったら	いこう	いけ
急ぐ	いそぎます	いそいで	いそいだ	いそがない	いそげる	いそげば	いそいだら	いそごう	いそげ
話します	はなします	はなして	はなした	はなさない	はなせる	はなせば	はなしたら	はなそう	はなせ
待つ	まちます	まって	まった	またない	まてる	まてば	まったら	まとう	まて
死ぬ	しにます	しんで	しんだ	しなない	しねる	しねば	しんだら	しのう	しね
遊ぶ	あそびます	あそんで	あそんだ	あそばない	あそべる	あそべば	あそんだら	あそぼう	あそべ
読む	よみます	よんで	よんだ	よまない	よめる	よめば	よんだら	よもう	よめ
取る	とります	とって	とった	とらない	とれる	とれば	とったら	とろう	とれ
走る	はしります	はしって	はしった	はしらない	はしれる	はしれば	はしったら	はしろう	はしれ
来る	きます	きて	きた	こない	これる こられる	くれば	きたら	こよう	こい
する	します	して	した	しない	できる	すれば	したら	しよう	しろ

Appendix C: Temporal Words

Months				**Days of the Months**
January	いちがつ		1st	ついたち
February	にがつ		2nd	ふつか
March	さんがつ		3rd	みっか
April	しがつ		4th	よっか
May	ごがつ		5th	いつか
June	ろくがつ		6th	むいか
July	しちがつ		7th	なのか
August	はちがつ		8th	ようか
September	くがつ		9th	ここのか
October	じゅうがつ		10th	とおか
November	じゅういちがつ		11th	じゅういちにち
December	じゅうにがつ		12th	じゅうににち
What month?	なんがつ？		13th	じゅうさんにち
			14th	**じゅうよっか**
Next Month	らいげつ		15th to 19th	(Same convention as 12th and 13th)
Last Month	せんげつ		20th	**はつか**
The month after next	さらいげつ		21st	にじゅういちにち
			24th	**にじゅうよっか**
			25th to 31st	(Same convention as 12th and 13th)

Days of the week			Friday	
Sunday	にちようび		Saturday	どようび
Monday	げつようび		What day is it?	なにようび？
Tuesday	かようび		Last Week	せんしゅう
Wednesday	すいようび		This Week	こんしゅう
Thursday	もくようび		Next Week	らいしゅう

Appendix D: Counters Reference

More Counters

つ	Used as part of the indigenous Japanese numbers 一つ, 二つ, 三つ etc.
とう	Large animals, cattle, elephants
ど	Occurrences, number of times, degrees of temperature or angle
ばん	Position, turn, sports matches
さい	Years of age
ひき	Small animals, insects, fish, reptiles, amphibians
びょう	Seconds
じ	Letters, kanji, kana, hours of the day
めい(Polite),にん	People
しゅう	Weeks
かこくご	Languages

Appendix E: Answers

Lesson 1: Practice
しちじです。
さんじです。

よじです。
はちじです。
じゅうじはんです。　・　じゅうじさんじゅっぷんです。
ごじはんです。・ごじさんじゅっぷんです。
ごじよんじゅっぷんです。
さんじさんじゅうごふんです。
はちじよんじゅっぷんです。
くじごじゅうごふんです。
しちじさんじゅうさんぷんです。
にじにじゅうにふんです。
いちじじゅういっぷんです。
ごぜんじゅういちじさんじゅうななふんです。
ごごろくじじゅうはっぷんです。
ごぜんじゅうにじよんじゅうよんふんです。

Lesson 2: Practice
つくえはあかいです。
いすはへやにあります。
はい、へやはおおきいです。

100
500
1100
200
ろっぴゃく
ななじゅうよん
さんびゃく
900
ごひゃくごじゅう
400
ななひゃく
せんさんびゃく

Create a Manga conversation (suggestion)

すみません、かばんはほんやにありますか。
いいえ、かばんはがっこうにあります。

Lesson 3: Practice
それは（or これは or あれは）なんですか？それは（or これは or あれは）けーたいです。
おてあらいはどちらですか？おてあらいはこちらです。
あのちかてつはとうきょうちかてつですか？いいえ、あれはしながわです。
そちらはだれですか？わたしのしゅじんです。

です
あります
います
です
います

Create a Manga conversation (suggestion)
ほてるにぎんこうがありますか？
いいえ、ぎんこうはえきのなかです。

Lesson 4: Practice
それはなんですか？せんせいのかんばんです。
そのほんはだれのほんですか？これはわたしのおくさんのほんです。
だいがくはとおいですか？いいえ、だいがくはちかいです。
わたしはまさおさんがすきです。

ごごしちじよんぷんです。
ごぜんじゅういちじごしゅうななふんです。
ごごよじさんじゅういっぷんです。
ごぜんじゅうにじよんじゅうはっふんです。

Lesson 5: この、その、あの
あの
これ
その
これ
(no answer required)
あっち

Create a Manga conversation (suggestion)
なにしますか？
ともだちとてれびをみます。
ともだちはあのはげのがいこくじんでしょう。
そうですよ。

(General practice, lessons 1 – 5)
てんきはあったかいです。だからやすみにします。まいけるさんとたなかさんととうきょうへいきます。
とうきょうはとおいですか。
いいえ、ちかいです。
でんしゃでいきますか。
いいえ、くるまでいきます。
とうきょうになにがありますか。
とうきょうにおおきいでぱーとがありますよ。
かばんとかさをかいます。
そのかばんはいくらですか。
ごひゃくえんですよ。
なんじにでますか。
こんばんのごじはんにでますよ。
あっおそいですね。
そうですよ。じゃ、いまいきますよ。
はい、ばいばい。
ばいばい。

Create a Manga conversation (suggestion)
てんきがわるいですよ。
かさがいりますね。あっ！　かさがありません。えきでかさをかいます。

Lesson 6:
いえにかえりました。
いえにかえりませんでした。
ろくじにねました。
ろくじにねませんでした。
すこしでした。
すこしじゃありませんでした。

Create a Manga conversation (suggestion)
けさおちゃをのみましたよ。おちゃはおいしいでしょう。あなたもおちゃのみますか？
いいえ、のみません。

あるーありますーありませんーありましたーありませんでしたーう Verb
ねるーねますーねませんーねましたーねませんでしたーる Verb
おきるーおきますーおきませんーおきましたーおきませんでしたーる Verb
いくーいきますーいきませんーいきましたーいきませんでしたーう Verb
よむーよみますーよみませんーよみましたーよみませんでしたーう Verb
くるーきますーきませんーきましたーきませんでしたーIrregular
するーしますーしませんーしましたーしませんでしたーIrregular
はなすーはなしますーはなしませんーはなしましたーはなしませんでしたーう Verb
みるーみますーみませんーみましたーみませんでしたーる Verb
かえるーかえりますーかえりませんーかえりましたーかえりませんでしたーう Verb
いただくーいただきますーいただきませんーいただきましたーいただきませんでしたーう Verb
はじまるーはじまりますーはじまりませんーはじまりましたーはじまりませんでしたーう Verb
べんきょうするーべんきょうしますーべんきょうしませんーべんきょうしましたーべんきょうしませんでしたーIrregular
すべるーすべりますーすべりませんーすべりましたーすべりませんでしたーう Verb

はい、ねます。いいえ、ねません。うん、ねる。いや、ねない。
はい、かえります。いいえ、かえりません。うん、かえる。いや、かえらない。
はい、します。いいえ、しません。うん、する。いや、しない。
はい、のみます。いいえ、のみません。うん、のむ。いや、のまない。
はい、みます。いいえ、みません。うん、みる。いや、みない。
はい、はじまります。いいえ、はじまりません。うん、はじまる。いや、はじまらない

Lesson 7:
にほん
よんぷん
ごまい

ななさつ
さんけん
はっかい
さんばい

いっさつーにさつーさんさつーごさつーななさつーきゅうさつ
いっぷんーにふんーさんぷんーごふんーななふんーきゅうふん
いっぽんーにほんーさんぼんーごほんーななほんーきゅうほん
いっかいーにかいーさんかいーごかいーななかいーきゅうかい
いっぱいーにはいーさんばいーごはいーななはいーきゅうはい

おとうさんはあんまりせがたかくありません。
わたしはあんまりねません。
わたしはあんまりほんをよみませんでした。

あのびるはいちばんたかいです。７２かいがあります。
いちばんたのしいです。
わたしのいえには 13 さつのまんがのほんがあります。

Create a Manga conversation (suggestion)
あなたのこうこうはおおきいですか？
はい、いちばんおおきいです。４かいまであります
ぼくのこうこうはもっとおおきいですよ。５かいまであります。

Lesson 8: Adjective Clauses
おわらないーおわらなかった
はじまらないーはじまらなかった
のまないーのまなかった
ふらないーふらなかった
みないーみなかった
たべないーたべなかった
しらべないーしらべなかった
でかけないーでかけなかった
くるまじゃないーくるまじゃなかった
しょうせつじゃないーしょうせつじゃなかった

こーひーをのまない。
みゆきさんにあわなかった。
えいごをしゃべらない。
それはにほんのはたじゃなかった。

そのひとはまさおさんのおとうさんじゃない。

（Adjectives）
とてもげんきないぬがいます。
けんじさんはきれいなかのじょがいます。
やすいこんぴゅーたをかいました。

わたしのくるまは・うるさかった・うるさかったです・うるさくない・うるさくありません・うるさくなかった・うるさくありませんでした
あのおとこのこは・せがたかかった・せがたかかったです・せがたかくない・せがたかくありません・せがたかくなかった・せがたかくありませんでした
わたしのいえは・しずかだった・しずかでした・しずかじゃない・しずかじゃありません・しずかじゃなかった・しずかじゃありませんでした
そのえんそうかいは・たのしかった・たのしかったです・たのしくない・たのしくありません・たのしくなかった・たのしくありませんでした

Create a Manga conversation (suggestion)
みちこちゃんのかばんはかわいいですね。
ありがとう。かわいくてやすかったよ。

はい、ながいえいがでした。
はい、やさしいせんせいです。
しろくてあかいまるがあるはたです。
やさしくてせがたかいひとです。
いいえ、テレビをみないひとです。

しずかなほてるでした。
きれいなかのじょでした。
げんきなこどもでした。
にぎやかながっこうでした。
おもしろくないえいがでした。
ひまなせんせいでした。

はやくあるきます。
たのしくはなします。
ていないにつかいます。

Lesson 9:
れぽーとをかいている。
くるまをなおしている。

わたしのかのじょがまっている。
あなたのおとうさんはどこでしたか？たべていた。

あそこでコーヒーをのんでいるひとがいます。
あそこでひるごはんをたべているひとがいます。
ここでべんきょうしているこどもがいます。
そこにこわれているくるまがあります。

これをよんでください。
ここでまってください。
ひろこをよんでください。

それをたべるとおもいます。
びるはあかいとおもいます。
かれはくるをいいました。
かのじょはぴあのをべんきょうしているといいました。

Create a Manga conversation (suggestion)
あのさかなはだいじょうぶ？いきていますか？
いいえ、しんでいますよ。

Lesson 10: Noun Modifiers
あそこででんしゃをまっているひとをよんでください。
あのすしをたべているでぶちゃんはみきさんのおとうとじゃありませんか？
おとうとはぼくがきのうすてたごはんをたべました。

おとうととみせへいってちゅごくごのほんをかいました。

やましたさんです	やましたさんだ
やましたさんでした	やましたさんだった
やましたさんじゃありませんでした	やましたさんじゃなかった

しずかです	しずかだ
しずかでした	しずかだった
しずかじゃありませんでした	しずかじゃなかった

そうです	そうだ
そうでした	そうだった

そうじゃありませんでした	そうじゃなかった

さきはいたみせ
このあいだとはんしたおばあさん
まちでみたじこ
きのうみたえいが
おおさかでとったびでお

わたしたちがはいたしょくどう
ぼくがみたえいが
ぼくがならったにほんご

これはさきはいたみせとちがいます
これはこのあいだとはんしたおばあさんとちがいます
これはまちでみたじことちがいます
これはきのうみたえいがとちがいます
これはおおさかでとったびでおとちがいます
これはわたしたちがはいたしょくどうとちがいます
これはぼくがみたえいがとちがいます
これはぼくがならったにほんごとちがいます

そのかさはこわれています。すてたほうがいいです。

てれびをみるのはおもしろいです。
ようふくをかうのはたのしいです。
すぺいんごをならうのはたいへんです。
おおさかのたべものをたべるのはおいしいです。

Create a Manga conversation (suggestion)
どうした？
よんでいるほんがわかりません。
あ、そう。まいにちよんでいる？
はい。よんでいますけどわかりません。
あ、そう。ぼくとべんきょうする？
はい。ありがとうございます。

Lesson 11:

あるく	Walk	あるける	あるけない
のる	Ride	のれる	のれない
のむ	Drink	のめる	のめない

つかう	Use	つかえる	つかえない
みせる	Show	みせられる	みせられない
よぶ	Call	よべる	よべない

てれびをみながらよるごはんをたべます。
でんしゃをのりながらけいたいをつかいます。
えいがをみながらともだちとはなします。
せんせいをききながらだいとうりょうになるゆめみます。

にほんごのじしょをよめますか。
にほんごでかけますか。
わたしのくるまをなおせますか。

ごぜんろくじにおきればおみやげをもらえます。
かのじょにでんわすればえいがをいくかもしれない。
そのおかしをたべればふとりますよ。

え、はやいかもしれない。
そうですね。いそがしいかもしれません。
え、うりけれたかもしれませんね。
そうですよ。なるかもしれない。

かれらはにほんごをはなせますか。
あのひとはせんぱいですか。え、せんぱいかもしれないよ。
わたしのけいたいでアメリカにかけますよ。
ばすをのりながられいきしをならえますね。

Lesson 12:
わたしのおにいさんはくるまをくれました。
しらないひとはいもうとにチョコレートをあげました。
"たなかさんはたんじょうびのためになんかをくれた？" （はい、ほんをくれました。）
いしかわくんがじぶんのかのじょにはなをあげた。

このれぽーとのこーぴーをあげます。
こうこうまでのせてあげる。
やってあげます。
はい、やってもらう。
はい、いずみさんとはなしてもらえませんか。
おかあさん、かみをきてくれる？

はい、けいさんしてあげます。
いただきます
ここへきてもらう。

(suggestions only, your answers may differ slightly, but still be correct)
くれました
もらいました
くれました
いただきました

げんきになってほしい。
こんぴゅーたーをとってもらいたい。
せんせい、すぴーちをしていただきたいのです。

まどをあけてもいいですか。
しゅくだいをしなくてもいいですか。
このくるまをここでちゅうしゃしてもかまいませんか。
まつもとしゃちょう、このかいぎをしゅっせきしてもかまいませんか。

さけをのんでみます。
いってみます。
かのじょをきいてみる。
くるまをなおしてみる。
てがみをかいてみます。

あげないとだめ	あげなければならない	あげなくてはならない・あげなくちゃ
よまないとだめ	よまなければならない	よまなくてはならない・よまなくちゃ
いわないとだめ	いわなければならない	いわなくてはならない・いわなくちゃ

Create a Manga conversation (suggestion)
あやちゃん、ケーキをつくってもらえませんか？
いいですけどざいりょうをかってほしいです。
でもくるまをもっていません。あなたのくるまをつかってかまいせんか？
いいですけどきをつけないとだめですよ。

(General Practice)
せんせい、きょう、はやくかえってもかまいませんか。

おてあらいをつかってもいいですか。
ぼくものってもいいですか。

らじおをけしてほしい。
いんたーねっとでしらべてもらいたいのです。
ここにとまってもかまいませんか。

おかあさんにでんわしないとだめです。
ぼくはもっとうんどうしないとだめです。
そのでんしゃをのらなければならない。

Final Review(Manga)
まさお：あのがいこくじんはだれ？
みゆき：まいけるです。アメリカからきたよ。
ひろこ：はじめましてひろこです。それはまさおとみゆきです。
まいける：はじめまして！いえにでんわをしないとだめ。けいたいをつかってもかまいませんか。
ひろこ：はい、いいですよ。ただ、アメリカにかけてはいけません。
まいける：ひひひ、アメリカじゃんくてほーむすてーにかけますよ。

ひろこ：さくらはきれいでしょう。
まいける：アメリカにもさくらがありますよ。
みゆき（まさおへ）：さくらのとなりまいけるとしゃしんをとってくれる？
まさお：はい。ところでアメリカのさくらはにほんからきたよ。
まいける：あそうですか。しらなかったよ。

あや：あしたのしけんをごうかく(pass)しなければならないよ。
みゆき：そうですよ。あさまでべんきょうしないとだめだよ。
まいける：あさまでべんきょうするとつかれてごうかくできませんね。
けんじ：れんしゅうのしけんをつくってあげるよ。
まいける：ありがとう！みゆき、ぼくのこたえ(answer)をかくにんしてくれる？
みゆき：ごめん、こたえはしりませんよ。あやにきいて！

ACKNOWLEDGEMENTS

When I first started this project, I had no idea of the months of work it would take me and many others to complete. I feel blessed to have people close to me who volunteered (or worked very cheaply) to help make this book a reality.

First, I owe so much to the talented illustrator, Kata Kane, for putting up with me, and creating the most amazing illustrations. It was like she was reading my mind. She also shared my vision, that is, we wanted the illustrations to not just tell a story and be entertaining, but to also help students learn Japanese faster. Thanks so much Kata!

I am also ingratiated to my four primary editors, Ms. Hiroko Mori, Mr. Kentaro Hara, Ms. Yoko Sonoda, and Mrs. Shiho Shimizu, all native Japanese from all walks of life who took time out of their busy schedules to carefully review the manuscript and point out mistakes. They also shared my vision to make the book relevant to contemporary Japan.

Lightning Source UK Ltd.
Milton Keynes UK
UKRC02n2346061116
287024UK00004B/15

Printed in Great Britain
by Amazon